I0149024

Journey Through
Pain To High Places

Christiana Agbor

© 2009 Christiana Agbor

All rights reserved. No part of this publication may be reproduced or transmitted in any form or by any means electronic or mechanical, including photocopy, recording, or any information storage and retrieval system, without permission in writing from both the copyright owner and the publisher.

Requests for permission to make copies of any part of this work should be mailed to Permissions Department, Witty Writings Publishing, LLC, 2875-F Northtowne Ln. #232 Reno, NV 89512

ISBN: 978-1-4276-1906-8

Printed in the United States of America by Witty Writings Press.

Acknowledgements

Heavenly Father,
I adore and revere you and truly confess
that without you I can do nothing.

Your love for me is unfathomable and indescribable.
Out of your grace and mercy you allowed me to be alive
today. I know I don't deserve to be here but
because of your forgiving power,
you have allowed me to see every new morning.
I appreciate all that you've done for me and
all that you will do according to your unfailing promises.

Thank you for allowing me to
go through the unbearable moments;
for leading me and healing me. Above all,
thank you for saving me through your son Jesus.
How can I love you in return for caring so much for me?
I feel blessed to have been given such a story
by the King of Kings to tell the world.
As I humbly testify in the name of my Healer, Friend and
Savior Jesus, who is my everything, I present this book to
you as a seed of my thanksgiving.

Until you call me home,
I'll forever adore and adorn you.

Your daughter,
Christiana

SPECIAL THANKS

To my family: My lovely father and mother, Joseph and Mary Agbor, my sister and brother-in-law Patricia and Raymond Ngata, Frida, Cecilia, Vivian, Agbor, Ako, Mado, and my niece, Claudia.

To all the doctors who were involved in my treatments: Dr. Timothy Dyches, Dr. Jonathan Tay, Dr. Schiff, Dr. Enohtanya, Dr. Mamouda K., Dr. Djomo, Dr. Ferris Gary, Dr. Cheryl Winder, Dr. Owen.

To my leaders in the Body of Christ: Reverend/Pastor Angela Acha-Morfaw, Pastor Chris Acha-Morfaw, Pastor Norris DuPree, Sr. and First Lady Remintha DuPree, Pastor Luther DuPree, Sr. and First Lady Jennifer DuPree, Reverend Dr. Umah Upkai, Pastor Chiori Vincent and Emana Chiori, Pastor Olubi Johnson, Prince Zilly Agrey, Pastor Mbah and First Lady Mirrielle, Mummy B, Elder Charles Enaw and Rosemary, Pastor Suh Ngeh Rambert and Vivian, Pastor William and Tony Ako.

To my family members in the Body of Christ: Pastor Nathan DuPree and Lady Denise DuPree, who were a true inspiration behind me writing my story, Minister Norris DuPree and Dr. Ireon DuPree, the family at Grace Tabernacle Church of God In Christ, Abundant Life Faith Center International, Korean Presbyterian Church, Sheila Etonga, Germaine Tezano, Ethel Nkwanyuo, Lovelyn Mundi, Jojo Salah, Senge Ekaney, Prysca Ngalame, Nadia Mahop, Crystelle Chimi, Nathalie Lowe, Betty and Dale Jasper, Ernest Lyonga, Emilienne Atia, Tabi .N. Enoh, Miatta Mbah.

To the following families: Agbor, Tataw, Atia, Eyong, Mbu-Ashu, Pounga, Lobe, Manga's of Atlanta, Georgia, Aiyuk of Reno, Nevada, Ako of Reno, Nevada, Alfred and Patience Tanyi.

To my editor: Kerri, for helping me tell my story.

Table of Contents

Introduction

A miraculous true story: revealing the essence of who God can be in your life. Many people experience God on different levels in their lives. This story will send chills down your spine and at the same time give you comfort as to what magnitude God can have in your life. It confirms that God is Jehovah Rapha, the One that healeth thee.

This story is like no other, revealing a young girl's struggle to find healing during the most difficult time of her life. In her search she finds more than she ever thought, the one and only true God: El Shaddai, the Almighty. When Christiana faced a devastating cancer in her life, she realized that no one could heal her except God. Jeremiah 17:14 says, "Heal me, Oh Lord, and I shall be healed; save me, and I shall be saved: for thou art my praise". She also realized that God is the one who wounds and He is also the one who heals (Deuteronomy 32:39). In search of a cure for her terrible disease, she heard a healing voice in the valley...

A Doctor's View

Christiana is a cancer survivor who is very unusual and rare in many ways, while at the same time being inspiring as well as rewarding to me as a physician. She was presented as a 23 year old African woman from Cameroon. Her age and country of origin in and of itself are unusual in my practice. She was diagnosed in Cameroon with a squamous cell carcinoma of the nasopharynx, after several years of being told she had allergies. She was told in Cameroon no treatments were available to her.

The age adjusted incidence of nasopharyngeal cancer varies in populations, but ranges from 28.8 per 100,000 in parts of China, to 17.2 per 100,000 in Eskimos, to 0.6 per 100,000 in the United States. The peak incidence is in the fourth and fifth decade of life, and males outnumber females by 3:1. Its incidence in West African nations is unknown. It is purported that in the Eskimo population nasopharyngeal cancer is caused by dimethylnitrosamine, found in high concentrations in salted fish which is a staple in the Eskimo diet. When salted fish is eaten, the diethylnitrosamine is aerosolized and found in high concentrations in the nasopharynx and nasal cavity. Interestingly, Christiana has a life-long history of smoked meats and fish in her diet. During my experience as a radiation oncology resident in San Francisco, I saw and treated many Chinese males with nasopharyngeal cancer, but never did I imagine I would treat it in a 23 year old West African woman.

Christiana's tumor was very advanced. It filled her nasopharynx and invaded her sinuses, skull base and cranial nerves, causing vision problems and headaches. In any typical nasopharyngeal cancer seen in the U.S., this type of presentation would seem incurable. Because of the survival benefit of chemotherapy when added to radiation, Christiana began a long, seven week course of radiation therapy and concurrent chemotherapy. Of all the body sites I treat in my practice, those in the head and neck area are some of the most difficult treatments for anyone to endure. To prevent serious dryness of the mouth, Christiana received 2 subcutaneous injections of amifostine in the abdomen daily before each radiation treatment. Amifostine is a selective radioprotector that accumulates in the salivary glands and protects them from the effects of radiation. With this treatment, dry mouth, loss of taste, severe sore throat and mouth, pain with swallowing, weight loss, fatigue, skin redness and peeling, nausea, vomiting and hypotension are all expected side effects. Detailed and sophisticated treatment planning was done to avoid radiation to critical structures such as the jaw, brain and optic chiasm, which, if irradiated too much, can result in blindness. Only with modern methods could we treat a tumor such as hers with a high a dosage while avoiding adjacent critical structures.

With perseverance and determination, Christiana was able to finish her treatment despite all of the terrible side effects. The end result was worth her effort, as the tumor melted away and was entirely gone shortly after the end of therapy. Her cranial nerve deficit resolved, and normal vision was restored.

Her story does not end there, however. Her nasopharyngeal cancer returned two more times: in September of 2004, the tumor showed up in her right femur and pelvic bones, and in January of 2006 the tumor showed up in her left femur and pelvic bones. Both recurrences were treated with more radiation therapy, and both times she had a complete response in pain relief as well as radiographically. In the meantime, she has no evidence of recurrence in the nasopharynx. Eight months later she remains free of disease.

Her battle with cancer is truly inspirational. Christiana, through all of her treatments, fought a battle to stay in the United States, and has now written this book about her experience while attending college with aspirations to receive a degree in pharmacy.

The course of her disease has not followed the typical natural course of nasopharyngeal cancer. After such a locally advanced primary tumor and two bony metastatic recurrences, one would not expect to see the patient as functional and aspiring as Christiana. I don't know if her success story is a result of the biology of her particular tumor, prayer and a miracle, or her bravery and attitude. I am grateful that I have shared this part of her life with her, and that I have her story to share with other patients who are early in their battle with cancer and need hope and inspiration.

Jonathan S. Tay, M.D.
(One of the doctors who treated Christiana in America)

** Written in September 2006 **

A Pastor's Witness

I found out that Christiana was sick through her sister Patricia Ngata, a member of our church. Patricia came to us asking for prayers for Christiana because it had been medically reported that she had an advanced stage of cancer. The prognosis of her condition was very bad and the treatment she needed was not available in her home country, Cameroon. As a body of Christ, we began to pray asking for God's divine intervention on her behalf. She desperately needed a miracle.

God answered our prayers as the first miracle happened when she first received her visa to come over to the United States. When she arrived, we continued our intercessions for her and God was faithful to continue the good work He had started. Then she came in contact with wonderful doctors and nurses who dedicated their time, extra concern and expertise on her case.

To cut a long story short on a Holy note, The Bible teaches us that all things are possible if we only believe. Witnessing all the phases of her healing was truly a blessing and testimony to the Body of Christ.

Today we can testify that through God's gracious intervention, Christiana is now made whole. Jehovah Rapha did it again and if He did it for Christiana, He can do it for you.

"Therefore I tell you, whatever you ask for

*in prayer, believe that you have received it,
and it will be yours."*

Mark 11:24 (NIV)

Norris DuPree, Sr.
Pastor, Grace Tabernacle Church of God in Christ
Sparks, Nevada

An Invitation

Christiana took Jesus for His word, just like the Centurion (Matthew 8:5-13). She argued, "If my Lord speaks the word, and the word only, I will be healed" – and she was healed!

Her testimony is "second to none". I dare you to read it.

Raymond Ngata
(Brother-in-law)

A Proven Faith

Christie is our special daughter in the Lord whose life we are grateful for. This authentic piece invites God's love, mercy, grace, healing and transforming power. Christie's testimony exemplifies a clear disbursement of faith out of a faith-crushing test. With her hope in the LORD, she overcame a devastating disease, cancer. Prospective readers, indeed, you are holding a faith amplifier and your faith will soar to limitless heights as you learn of her miracle. Undoubtedly, once you begin reading this book, you won't stop! It is our utmost prayer that you testify to the Glory of God too!

> *"And they overcame him [the devil] by the blood of the Lamb, and by the word of their testimony; and they loved not their lives unto the death."*
>
> Revelation 12:11(KJV)

Prophet Charles and Dr. Rosemary Enaw

An Answered Prayer

I first met Christiana (or Baby Tina, as I call her), one Tuesday when she came for counseling and prayers. As I talked with her, it turned out that she was a member of our church. It was a fairly large and growing congregation, so it was understandable that I had not noticed her. However, I got to know she was the sister of a close friend of mine, Cecilia. When I sought to know what had brought her to church that morning, she told me she had been complaining of nasal congestion for quite some time. She was also beginning to lose her hearing. The doctors did not know what was wrong with her. I gave her some Psalms to read and meditate on, prayed for her, and urged her to attend the miracle service which would be held the very next Thursday.

That Thursday during the service, I prayed and anointed her with oil, in accordance with the word of God. The next Monday, she went back to the hospital, and for the first time in over five years, the doctors were able to discover that she had an advanced stage of cancer. When I heard this I realized that she really needed prayers. Everybody knows that cancer has no cure, but I knew that God could cure not just cancer, but any other sickness or disease. We began to intercede for her. It was at this point that another miracle happened. She had earlier applied for a visa to travel to the United States, which had been denied. When she went back, the same interviewer who had denied her visa now approved it for her.

Some years later, I came to the United States and was privileged to preach at Grace Tabernacle Church where

21

Tina worshipped. When I saw her, I knew that something had happened in her life. Her vision had been corrected, her hearing restored, and she was completely cancer free. I just gave God the glory. This was His handiwork. All I had done was give the word with which He perfected her healing.

Some people say they do not believe in the healing power of God. Well, Tina is an eloquent testimony to the fact that God does indeed heal. I believe that her healing began when we interceded on her behalf, and a situation that had baffled doctors for years was easily diagnosed. The combination of faith and medication was able to perfect her healing. It does not matter of what nature the sickness or disease is. If He did it for her He can do it for anyone out there who can dare to believe in Him for healing. It could be physical, emotional, or spiritual. It makes no difference to Him. He can heal them all.

I know that the book you are holding in your hands is the point of contact you need to reach out to God for your complete and total healing and restoration.

You will also have a testimony, in Jesus' name. Amen!

Rev. Angela Acha-Morfaw
Senior Pastor, Abundant Life Faith Chapel International
Yaoundé , Cameroon

A Miraculous Testimony

The testimonies have begun…

> *"And these signs shall follow them that believe, in my name they shall cast out devils; they shall speak with new tongues; They shall take up serpents; and if they drink any deadly thing, it shall not hurt them; they shall lay hands on the sick and they shall recover".*
>
> Mark 16:17-18 (KJV)

> *"He sent his word and healed them, and delivered them from their destructions".*
>
> Psalm 107:20 (KJV)

It is an honor and a privilege to testify of my healing from breast cancer, which resulted from obedience on Sister Christie's part. To understand the magnitude of this healing, it is important to give the background on which this miracle was set.

I am presently a pediatric oncologist. I became born again soon after completing medical school in Nigeria, West Africa in 1994. Needless to say my training and experience with health catastrophes and death amongst patients who confessed faith was diametrically opposed to what the word of God has to say on the subject. In summary, I was set up for doubt and unbelief. Everything else concerning the benefits of the cross and the Lord's crucifixion I received, except for healing. Oh, did I know the scriptures and quote them! Yet there was a spiritual disconnection between my head and my heart.

After immigrating to the United States about 18 months later, I married my high school sweetheart. I continued to grow in the Lord and He gave me the land to possess. I began medical residency training in pediatrics a few years later. During my internship (first) year, I gave birth to our beautiful first daughter; only for her to be diagnosed with sickle cell anemia (a blood disorder which predominantly affects people of African descent). Now my faith concerning healing was all the more challenged. I cried, I prayed for healing, but did not get the 'Rhema' word. Needless to say, she had multiple problems with seven hospitalizations in her second to fourth year of life.

Seven years later, and at 37 years of age, I became pregnant with our third child. Persistent breast tenderness led me to seek the consultation of a surgeon. The biopsy confirmed infiltrative ductal carcinoma of the right breast: there was no lymph node involvement and three lesions were found at surgery. I rejoiced the Lord helped me "catch it early". Not so! My medical-knowledge-driven faith limits Him, the most High, to only be able to save me from spread.

In between my first and third child, I can now see clearly how the Lord was preparing me and creating a door of escape. He opened the door for pediatric training and then ordered my steps to sub-specialize in oncology. I have seen affliction, suffering and death from aggressive cancers. Now following the birth of my baby, staging work up by CT and bone scans showed spread! I had 18 small lesions in both lungs and another lesion in one of my ribs! Distant metastasis (spread)? Horrible! Needless to say, my knowledge of oncology, and the medical facts superseded the truth of the healing word of God that had not yet become Rhema to me. As I began to "set my house in order", many people stood in the gap and interceded for me (siblings, friends and prayer partners). Yet, I could not make it past the spiritual disconnection of fact and truth!

Then on July 4th 2007, Sister Christie calls, with a conviction and an unction that could only be the Holy Ghost. As she prays and speaks the Word (none new) there is a supernatural transmission from head to heart. The Word becomes alive and literally quickens my mortal body. I am awestruck! She declares I shall not die, but live to declare the works of the Lord in the land of the living. She reminds me of the story of Hezekiah and implores the Lord to overturn the judgment. Suddenly, the words take on life and become Rhema! That night I moved from death to life. I have since then completed chemotherapy and subsequent scans reveal no sign of cancer!!!

I declare with my mouth that I shall have forty more years to show forth His glory. Already, all my colleagues are already amazed at how well I've done and I have the opportunity to be a witness. I am blessed to have had Sister Christie call me and I know I'll live fully because of her obedience. I hope her testimony blesses you. She is walking in *dunamis* power!

Elna Saah, M.D.

*** Written in January 2008 ***

Chapter 1
Misplaced Passion

*Train a child in the way he should go and
when he is old he will not turn from it.*

Proverbs 22:6(NIV)

Going to America is almost every African child's
dream and was mine as well. Far back at the age of seven,
I was dressed in my best outfit sitting on the edge of the
bed with my older sister Mado, who had also been fooled
by an in-law of ours, who'd told us we were going to travel
on the plane with her. Thinking it was true we sat on the
bed waiting for the plane to come for us. Our firm
decisions to stay awake were defeated when we fell asleep.
We got up in the morning and realized we were still in
Cameroon and that our in-law had traveled to the United
States without us.

We never stopped hoping to go to America. Every
time we heard the sound of a traveling plane, we rushed
outside to take a look at it. We always thought our
president was on the plane. We never deciphered if it was
coming into the country or leaving. All we knew was that
the plane was traveling abroad with President Paul Biya of
Cameroon in it. How we longed to just see what a plane
looked like inside. Each time we went to the airport, I felt
like I was somewhere outside of my country. I kept writing
letters to our relatives expressing my desire to go to
America. I wore clothes and shoes from America. Each
time I was dressed in a Made-In-America outfit, I knew no
one in my country could have it and I could not wait to get

27

to church to receive complements for it. It made me feel cute and outstanding. America to me was the place where manna still fell from heaven and everything was bright and fair. I had in mind that as soon as one arrived in America, one could command the heavens to drop the finest things on earth and it would happen. America was very much flowery as the object of my favorite childhood imagination.

When I was ten years old I was promoted to secondary school. Skipping one class in primary school was so exciting but leaving some friends behind was not very easy to deal with. On the day before I left for Saker Baptist College, I found it worthy to visit one of my friends to bid her good-bye. On my way to her vicinity, I decided to take a short cut I had never passed through before. As I walked further, I noticed I was getting into a more isolated and densely forested area. I debated within about continuing in the same track, but looking back it seemed too long a journey to consider, so I kept going.

In the middle of the forest, I realized there was a man following me and as I tried to walk faster, he began walking faster too. I could hear his footsteps and feel his presence behind me. I did not want to look behind but I could feel a dangerous presence. No house was nearby. No one was around in case I cried out for help, and there was no other route besides that one. All of a sudden, I started mumbling the first verse of the prayer that my mom obligated me to read every night, Psalm 23: "The Lord is my shepherd, I shall not want". The man asked me if I was in the stage of my womanhood. I did not fully understand at first, but then I perceived what he meant. I knew he was bad but I kept mumbling and walking faster. I was afraid that he was a killer or thief. My heart beat faster than ever;

thank God he did not touch me. He just kept talking and all my responses were brief and "no" or "je ne sais pas", that is, I do not know in French.

After walking for about ten minutes through that forest I saw the outlet to the road where people and cars passed. I realized he was still on my route until I got close to where my friend's house was. The man tapped my hip and said bye. From there he took another route. I said thank God. When I got to my friend's house, I narrated the story to her but as soon as we started playing, I forgot about it.

Years later, I now realize that the Lord truly was my shepherd because that man had the chance to take advantage of my innocence in any way; either kill, steal or abuse me. He was certainly Satan's employee.

On my way back to the house, I automatically took the longer road so I could walk in the midst of many people in the broad daylight. It is the same way with our walk with Christ in this world. We all have taken shortcuts in life, either through lying, stealing, etc. No one drinks to get drunk but sometimes that is the end result. I remember seeing a drunken man giving all of his money to a lady he did not know at a bar. No one likes to see things go this way, but why not change your route? God may have protected us from the dangers we passed, but what about taking another road?

Many years ago, my cousins and I had stolen my uncle's cooked beans. We intended to have just a taste but ended up eating all of it. We were yet hungry again and after cooking the dog's food, which was a pot of meat, we ate some of it too. We prayed for my aunt to forget about the beans, but the following morning, my uncle asked for it and I pretended to search for it. Of course it was nowhere to be found. When I voiced that I could not find it, it was strange. Right away my uncle thought that the most mischievous person in the house had eaten it, so he went and asked my younger cousin Tina who fearfully admitted the truth. He came back to me expecting that "most honest Christie" would tell the truth. Without knowing that he had already found out the truth, I told him I did not know. Right away he called my cousin to confess in front of all of us. Oh what an embarrassment and shame it was! I had been trusted because of my honesty in the past but what about that day? We all hate to be called liars and thieves. Yet we thought if you lied without being caught then it was alright, but before we even confessed, we were already liars.

> *"If we claim we have not sinned, we make him out to be a liar and his word has no place in our lives"*
>
> 1 John 1:10 (NIV)

My ignorance and fantasy about America did not fade when I became an adolescent. My dad had always talked of sending his children to further their studies abroad, but faith without works made that idea dead. Papa's plan was to have us travel according to our birth sequence, from the oldest to the youngest. My oldest sister Patricia had left for the United States in the 1980's but after that, traveling agendas did not seem to work out again for us. I was the seventh out of eight children in the family. My turn to travel was not anywhere near. Although many were the plans in my dad's heart, God's reply was final. If my dad was asked who was next on his list to travel, my older sisters names would have been mentioned first. In high school, a classmate heightened her ambition to go to America as she would always say "when we get to America then we will know we have accomplished our mission on earth". That was great imagination, but the passion we ought to have had for heaven was misplaced with America. My dream did not die. I just did not know how and when I was ever going to see America.

My mother always took us to church. I was a passionate member of the Presbyterian Christian youth group. It was a custom to recite Bible scriptures on Christmas day and act out the scene of baby Jesus in the manger. My parents chose to send my siblings and I to Christian schools where the word of God was the foundation. I went through all the training yet still hadn't surrendered my life to Christ and I was ignorant about the anointing. The only part of the Bible I mastered was the book of Revelation, particularly the part describing 666 and the mark of the beast. Hey, that was scary.

Once an alarm was made by some students in the secondary school I attended that Jesus was on His way back to earth for judgment. One of my buddies named Jojo, who was a fan of secular music, came telling me that she believed Jesus was coming soon. Out of fear she threw away all her tapes and surrendered her life to Christ. That shocked me and made me think that if Jojo of all people had believed, then why not me? Out of fear that Jesus would come soon, I also surrendered and started consuming my mind with praises to God.

We got into a so-called fasting period with lots of other classmates who had also been saved. We were starving ourselves and thought we were fasting. Many of us did not know what it meant to fast. Some senior students tried to get us out of that, and we were overjoyed, thinking we were experiencing persecution. When the news got back to the school authority that there was a group of students who had gone days without eating, the principal addressed us and slowly we realized we were not doing the right thing. I particularly was not doing the right thing but I really cannot talk about what others thought. I was really hungry and did not have an aim for fasting.

I thought fasting meant going days without food and the more you resisted hunger, the more righteous you were. I thought if Jesus came at that time I would have been a candidate for heaven. These were pure lies because I was driven by fear, trying to be overly righteous, which is also a sin. I never knew that man's righteousness was like filthy rags. One day I forgot about fasting and thirst prompted me and a friend to grab a bottle of water. As we drank a bit of it, she quickly said, "Christie, we forgot we were fasting". We both spat the little left in our mouth and started confessing to God, but what about the water in our belly? Though we strive to live a perfect life we must always acknowledge we are made righteous by grace, which is the death and resurrection of Jesus Christ.

As an adolescent, I was not kingdom minded but I followed my older sister to church on Sundays. I watched how people fell under the anointing. I did not know what that was and felt it was exaggerated drama. It was disgraceful to cry out in the midst of people. I was so concerned about the people. Why should people allow tears to stream down their faces in front of an audience? I never understood they were crying out to God and did not know there was a scripture, "A broken and a contrite heart is what God desires" (Psalm 51:17). To me, they fell all by themselves or were pushed down by the pastor.

I was more of a spectator in church. I prayed hard never to cry or fall down like those other people, which was ludicrous. Every announcement in the church was a recitation to me. Whenever the Elder Ewane announced that anyone who needed special prayers should see the pastor on Tuesday, I prayed that he would rapidly end his speech and get off the pulpit so praise time could come and I could show off my dancing skills. Seeing the pastor on the pulpit on Sunday was enough, why would people want to meet the pastor on another day? That did not make sense to me at the time. I thought prayer could be a repeated rhetorical legend instead of asking someone else to pray for you. What difference would that make? I was totally ignorant of the scripture "The effectual fervent prayers of the righteous availeth much" (James 5:16).

Worship did not mean a thing to me. The church was meant for me to visit only on Sundays. I loved to sit at the back of the church where I could make some noise, gossip, approve of people's countenance or outfit, take note if they repeated their shoes and clothes from last Sunday or sleep during the sermon without being noticed. Again, for me the front seats were meant for the overly religious and watchmen of the church. Why did people rush to go to church, did that even matter? The church was a building and socializing arena to me. The word of God was like a fairy tale that was recounted over and over. I listened to it but never heard a thing. The Holy Spirit never existed in my vocabulary. I knew about God and Jesus only and that was enough.

I could recite Psalm 23 by heart, thanks to my mom who made me recite it every night before I went to sleep. I knew nothing about the Holy Trinity. Were your parents as hard on you when it came to God's business? In all of my parents' conversations, the beginning and the end was about God. They did the best they could to protect us. We spent most holidays at home while other children came over to visit us. Still our parents were not flexible about approving our requests to attend even neighborhood birthday parties.

I remember we were invited to a neighbor's birthday party and because no one was available to accompany us, we were sent to drop off a gift and return to the house. My dad denied our request to go because neither he nor my mother would be around. We could hear the surging music and the noise of the kids and that made me feel like I was missing out on the ambiance. I never understood that my dad's refusal was based on the fact that no one from the house was going to be with us. One Sunday, the celebrant's mother saw me on the playground and asked why we did not come to the birthday party. In my childish honesty I said, "My dad refused, he said we should not attend". I do not know how this ended but she came to understand the matter.

While in primary school, each time my cousin Sheila and her mom visited, I begged her to tell my dad that she wanted me over for the weekend. She was so eloquent and my dad always gave her a positive response which worked well for us as we planned to play a lot. My parents did a good job trying to protect us, but when I got to the university I had the chance to decide whether to stroll around on Sundays or go to church. I went to church when others went but chose not to go most times. Nevertheless, my parent's effort did not go in vain because the Bible says if you teach a child the way he should go, when he grows up he will not depart from it. It does not matter how long your loved one lingers away, the truth is they will not depart because eventually every knee shall bow and every tongue will confess that Jesus is Lord.

Chapter 2
God is the Giver of Sleep

At the age of five I had been sick with pneumonia and bronchitis, both of which were treated until I went to secondary school and began snoring at night. That was interpreted as a sign of tiredness but when I went to high school my snoring became even louder. I could be heard snoring far off from where I slept. In high school I could never nap during break time in class because snoring was very much considered a male thing and not for a girl. It was disgraceful for a girl to snore. I always had to breathe through my mouth. My hands trembled all the time as though I was nervous. It was attributed to the coffee I drank so I could stay awake to study all night.

At night, I was always the last to fall asleep because slumber did not come easily. I grew tired of breathing through my mouth and complained to the school doctor who said I was suffering from anxiety and referred me to the school chaplain for prayer. At the time I knew anxiety had to do with the word "hurry" and that irritated me. I was unsatisfied with the doctor's diagnosis but went to see the chaplain anyhow. In my mind I thought, "How will prayer help? How could I be sick and not prescribed any medication?" When I got to the chaplain's office, he asked what I feared most and I thought he had completely misunderstood my problem. I grumbled within to get out of his office while he said a prayer that I don't remember except for the Amen.

I kept complaining in school about my breathing difficulties until I was granted an exit to go home. When I carried the complaint home, based on the fact that the latter doctor was unable to say what was exactly wrong, it sounded like I was over-exaggerating. One of my sisters told me, "Christie, if school has become too tough, pack your belongings and come home". At this point I thought I had complained enough, because no one understood my pain. I decided to stop talking about it, accept my pain and return to school.

One night as I bent my head to study, blood started gushing out of my nostrils. If it had been in the day time it would have been said I had a nosebleed because of the sun, but I had never had a nosebleed before. I rushed to the school dispensary and laid there for some time until the bleeding ceased. It created an eerie feeling within. What was it? The doctors did not know and neither did I. Who was going to tell me what was wrong? Like the man at the pool of Bethesda, if Jesus would have appeared before me then and asked, "Would you be made whole?" my answer would have been, "I have no doctor who is able to diagnose what is wrong". I needed God's intervention but did not know how to claim my healing because I did not study the Bible. I was totally ignorant of the fact that God could reach out to me. My reliance was completely pivoted around any doctor's report.

My uncle had expressed my complaints to one of his friends who worked in the medical field. Without examining me, his friend assumed what I could be suffering from and prescribed some medication over the phone. How unwise that was. Just because someone is coughing does not mean cough syrup will work for them and just because someone is crying that does not mean they have just lost a loved one. Nevertheless, I took the medication but there was no change or even a break in my sickness. After this, I stopped complaining because my mind was settled that no one understood how I was hurting so I tucked my complaint within.

My only witnesses were classmates who were aware of the weird snoring and the involuntary flow of blood out of my mouth and nose at the same time. That was scary to see and they told me I needed to go home to seek more medical advice. None of them knew that it was no better at home. My dad came up with his own remedy, assuming it was just some kind of cold. My family had never witnessed the bleeding scenario. I tried to complain again, yet to no avail, so I stopped complaining because I did not want to hear anyone tell me I was trying to avoid school work.

I don't know how I managed to study at all. I was always tired because I constantly breathed through my mouth. If I climbed a short staircase, I felt like I was going to faint. I never played any sports because my health did not permit me. I barely made it through high school, and that was only by the grace of God.

Months before I attended high school I stayed in my uncle's house with my two cousins for a short period of time. We knew night outings were not accepted so we decided to sneak out. We monitored my aunt and uncle's movements and made our own plans to leave once they fell asleep. That night it seemed like they lingered around the parlor longer than usual. It was 9:00pm and we had to leave so I called our little cousin Sophia to shut the door behind me as I left to join my two cousins. She was so drowsy that she never shut it.

We had to jump over a fence into our neighbor's farm. My cousins were both taller than I, so jumping over was not a problem for them. The fence was uneven and the lowest part of it was directly opposite the louvers of my aunt's room. If she had looked out the window, she would have caught us. It took me a while because it was my first time trying to jump over a fence. My cousins grumbled as I slowly struggled to climb. Finally, one of them had to help me out. As I made it over someone was standing there, I suppose one of the neighbor's sons. He did not know our names and as he stretched his hand trying to use sign language to stop us, we ran away like we had never seen him.

When my peers saw me, they were so glad and amazed that I was in their midst. They all asked how I made it there because I was known to live in a very strict home where night visits were never accepted. Ten minutes after we made it to the party, the MC (Master of Ceremony) loudly called out our names on his microphone. "Miss Christie Agbor you are urgently needed out of this party by your uncle". I heard the crowd boo.

Our uncle was outside waiting for us with a stick in his hand, a friend reported. I acted as though I was not one of those who had been called out, although I trembled greatly within. When I noticed that people were distracted with dancing, my friends thought of hiding me in the DJ's little room. Nevertheless, once I got home, we were seriously reprimanded. When this story was recounted to my dad, it was no fun. I was warned to never repeat that behavior again. Later, I succeeded in high school but that did not cover up my dad's rage. It was more important to him to have a good name, more than any accomplishment (Proverbs 22:1). A good name is better than gold and silver. I thank God for touching the hearts of my aunt and uncle who later forgave me.

That ugly incident always seemed to flash back from time to time. While reading one of our literature books, "I Will Marry When I Want" by Nguki and Nguki, my teacher Mr. Quan hinted to the class that I could better tell them what it meant to sneak out at night. I was embarrassed that he knew. Hallelujah, the class ended right as he called for me to tell my story. Apparently someone had told him about what I had done.

I visited all my friends in the neighboring areas before I left for the far off university I attended. On one of my visits, we decided to get some food and drinks in a restaurant. As we chatted we heard a weird sound like a gunshot from an unknown direction, "kwooh kwooh kwooh" was the sound.

Everyone in the restaurant fell flat on the floor. People jammed into each other, fell on tables and had accidents. Not too long after that, the police surrounded the area. No one could tell what it was. Situations like that are very uncommon in Cameroon, which has a reputation for being the most peaceful African nation. The atmosphere returned to normal as people burst out laughing and commenting. Tables were on the floor and things were in disarray. What if it was an unexpected scene? What would have been my explanation? What was I doing there? I was supposed to have been traveling to school. I don't think

God wanted me there. I was not fit to be in such environments, I did not belong there. I decided to leave out of fear.

Sometimes situations cause us to leave places and separate us from people after which we ponder why and how we left. God allows some situations to reveal the plans the enemy has for us while showing His protection in order to position us in alignment with His plan for our life. In every milieu that we find ourselves, it is worth asking if God is a partaker of our company and purpose for being there, without which we may be in the wrong place. One should be witnessing in the midst of unbelievers while allowing the light of God to shine so others can see God's good work and bring glory to His name.

If Abraham had stayed with his family, he would have been in the wrong company for the will of God for his life. Though he kindheartedly took his nephew Lot, God's original plan was for him to leave his entire family behind (including Lot). Separation is not enmity.

I attended university in the western part of my country which is very cold. When I woke up in the mornings after tossing and turning all night, I felt like I had just carried logs of wood. I was so frustrated and tired that I spent most mornings in bed. I did not go to class because I was in such pain and really felt sick. I sent a message through one of my cousins, Agatha, who was traveling to the central province where my sister resided to tell her that I was not feeling well. Agatha returned with a message from my sister saying there was no way she could help because she had no money at the time. Blood kept gushing out of my nostrils in the morning hours, yet amazingly it never occurred in the presence of any of my siblings or parents. All they heard were my complaints.

A certain professor's wife advised me to quit the university and take care of my health. She did not know what was happening on the other side, where no doctor had been able to diagnose my condition and my family could not understand anything. It was unusual to complain about an ailment, have the doctors examine you and then not have a diagnosis. Since we never experienced such a difficult situation in my family, I had to deal with the inexplicable pain and confusion alone.

Many medications are sold in my country without a prescription. By my own reasoning, I took any medication I could find that had to do with the ear, nose, throat or sinuses. I even went as far as taking overdoses just so I could have some sleep. Still, sleep did not come effortlessly.

I hated the location of the university and its climate. Since I complained so much with no medical evidence to back my complaints and had expressed my dislike for the vicinity of the school, it really could not be understood that I was truly sick. In my family's opinion everything boiled down to the fact that I did not want to study in that part of the country. I absolutely did not want to be there and so I lost the zeal to study. I was mad because I could not bring myself to go to class and most of my classes were in the morning hours. It was hard for anyone to understand that I struggled to wake up in the morning. I never slept enough and could not fall asleep when I wanted to. I was dying in silence and no one was able to understand my cry. Everything was associated to juvenile behavior, which was partly true.   Absenteeism was noted and failure was evident.   My absence from school set an alarm and my sisters finally had me out of there to return home.

My passion had been to work in the communication field. Once I succeeded in getting into the advanced school of communication I thought the puzzle of my life had been well fitted but now the underlying issues needed to be taken care of. My health had not improved as the same symptoms could still be noticed. Now it came to full understanding that I was not trying to dramatize my situation as it was obvious there was no way I could study in bad health.

One day blood suddenly started gushing out of my nostrils again and my sister Cecilia saw it for the first time. The nosebleeds had become normal for me and I knew it would stop eventually. As I lay on the bed waiting for the bleeding to stop she began interceding in prayer and speaking in tongues. Another time my other sister Frida spent the night with me and she complained that she could not sleep because I snored so loud. I was urged to seek another doctor's advice and when we got to this ear, nose and throat specialist's office, he looked through my nostrils and could not see clearly so he requested an x-ray. He insisted on having the results that same day. When we presented the films to him, he diagnosed me with chronic sinusitis and said my nostrils needed to be drained. He prescribed some medications that go along with the draining process.

On our way to the pharmacy, we met one of Frida's friends, Martine, who inquired why we were on our way to get medications. She asked for the name of the doctor who was going to do the drainage. When my sister told her she stopped us right away and narrated a story about how this same doctor had carelessly treated her cousin, who was taken to Paris for more treatment and later died because one of his nerves had been mistakenly touched. She told us this doctor tied the legs and hands of his patients in order to perform the drainage. If the patient was a little unsteady while the drainage went on, he was harshly scolded to get steady. That was scary enough to forget about him.

The next day, we were referred to another ear, nose and throat specialist, and so we consulted the next proposed doctor. We took along the x-ray films from the previous visit and this other doctor blasted the diagnoses of the other doctor. He said the films from the previous hospital were not clear enough for anyone to make any analysis. He asked for the repetition of new films in a different location. We came back with the new films and when he looked at them, he said there was evidence of a nose blockage but he did not know what that was. He even went ahead to say if the previous doctor had performed drainage, I probably would have bled to death. He confessed that it was not right to push aside the diagnoses of another doctor but that he could not help but tell us the truth. He explained that it could be an unknown allergy. He then prescribed some medications and asked me to try them and come back in one month.

Undoubtedly, we realized the former doctor's report was not right and God had used Frida's friend to block the risk of me dying. Frida got my prescribed medications and I took them as required for a month, after which I returned to the doctor's office for a checkup. He affirmed there was no improvement and after about four visits with different medications, it looked more to Frida like an experimental try.

I still could not breathe through my nostrils and I continued to snore. Frida thought this doctor was an honest one but his testing was taking too long to reach a conclusion. More so, he had seen a tiny piece of cotton in my eardrum and said we needed to pay extra money for him to remove it. I then remembered that three years earlier, cotton from a Q-tip had slipped and stuck in my ear. I called a nearby nurse to help remove it, but she only succeeded in taking out a little piece. Since she could not see the interior of my ear, she thought she had removed all of it. Several times I cleaned my ears and could not feel the cotton. Frida understood that my condition was a tough one and suggested we go to another renowned hospital.

At the next hospital, we consulted a French doctor who had just come from Paris. After requesting additional x-ray films, he also said there was a nose obstruction however he did not know exactly what it was. He also said it could be an allergy. He removed the piece of cotton from my ear without extra charge. This doctor made a difference as I noticed he was more concerned with the diagnosis than the money. Though we still had to confirm payment before any work started, his priority was to first get my complaints. His diagnosis was very much like the previous doctor's analysis. He prescribed medications, which I took. When I went back to consult, he repeatedly gave me the same medications and altered his prescriptions only a little. I was constantly having x-rays done and taking medications which did not help.

When I came for one of my checkup appointments, the receptionist told me he returned to Paris and another doctor had replaced him. I consulted the new doctor who requested an x-ray after which he diagnosed that I was suffering from trauma. This was very much unheard of so I asked if he could refer me to another doctor closer to where I was living, of which he did. I was excited to meet a new doctor and have medical students use my case in their study. This time it was fun because I knew one of them.

I went to this new doctor's office several times, yet the medications he prescribed were not making any difference either. He also requested x-rays and the films were not clear enough for him to see what was wrong with me, so he kept requesting repeated x-rays to be taken. On one visit, the radiologist became frustrated because he thought the doctor was sending him too many messages of a job poorly done. He angrily told me that I would have to shave off my hair down to the roots for the films to properly reflect what was hiding in my nostrils. This sounded funny to me because I was nowhere close to having a haircut. It would not have happened.

This latest doctor sent me to one of his colleagues to examine my ears because I had ringing in my ears. His colleague did a hearing test and evaluated that I was fast losing the hearing in my left ear but the cause of all of these problems was still unknown. The results were sent back to my doctor and when he saw them, he prescribed more medication.

Worse still, on a certain afternoon I was dressed, deodorized, perfumed and all set to go out. As I was about to step out, Frida was coming back from work and she smelled an unusual odor and quickly expressed dislike for such a pungent smell. She said I smelled like I was freshly from the shower but some odd smell diffused in the living room. She smartly suspected it was from my nose and when she looked into my nostrils, she realized that it stunk even more. She bluntly said there was no way I could step out in such stink until we consulted the doctor again. This was on a Friday and I could only visit the doctor on Monday. On Sunday she advised that I sit near the entrance of the church and alert those who sat beside me that my breath stunk.

I could not stand people with mouth or body odor. If I came across anyone in that situation, I made sure they saw that I could not stand their odor as I would almost puke in this kind of atmosphere, but this time it was me. How could I run away from me?

On Monday, I consulted my doctor and he requested a biopsy to be done at another hospital by another doctor. I was getting tired of everything because I still could not breathe well, sleep well nor hear well. Prayer was still a recitation to me but I had never really thought that God was actually listening to me and that He could respond.

Chapter 3
The Word of God is Not a Legend

One of my friends had picked up a paper which instructed that at the mention of the "Hail Mary" prayer forty times, you could ask for anything you wanted and it would be granted to you. I was not a Catholic but I quickly bought the idea. I prayed the "Hail Mary, full of grace" prayer about forty times and commanded ten things I wanted; amongst which was my healing and request to travel to America, as instructed by the paper. Though nothing good happened, I continued to have hope. Another friend borrowed the prayer after which she said it was missing, but we thought she had hidden it from us so she could read it every day. I followed up so she could find it because I so badly needed my request to be answered. Thank God it was never found and I soon forgot about it.

All I knew was to read the Psalms. In my mind the Bible was a book of old times we had just to keep the old tradition of reading it. I did not know what it meant to have a personal relationship with God. I continued to sit in the back of the church with my friends where we could make some noise, dance and have a proper view of people as they went to the offering basket.

Cecilia advised me to go see the pastor for prayers on Tuesday. When I met Pastor Angela Acha-Morfaw, she was so shocked that I was Cecilia's younger sister and that she had never met me. Well, the church was massively populated and I always sat at the back. That reminded me of my first visit to the church. First-timers were given a form to fill out, but I had folded mine and put it in my hand bag. Consequently, I was seen but not known. This time I discovered for myself why people needed prayers. The Pastor asked me to come for miracle service on Thursday and I attended unfailingly. She prayed for me, anointed me with oil and laid hands on me. Tears streamed down my face but I did not know why. I thought I'd had enough of everything and meeting the Pastor was my last resort.

On the following week, I went to another doctor who was to carry out the biopsy. When I got to his office, I could identify the same instruments all the other doctors had used, but this time I had my Bible with me. He carried on with the same procedure of sticking cotton in my nostrils that had been deepened in some medication to provide a better view. Usually after about five minutes, it was taken out and my nostrils were examined. This time the outcome was different with Doctor Kouotou. God had been invited to help and He showed up. It is one thing to know God has promises for you and it is another thing to claim or receive the promises. I passively knew God was a Healer but I did not know I had to reach out to Him to receive my healing.

When he removed the cotton from my nostrils, blood streamed out. No previous doctor ever had this amazing result before. I didn't even know what the flow of blood meant. All I heard the doctor say was "ca commences bien" which means "here comes a good start". He began using scissor–like instruments to remove white bead-shaped stuff from my nostrils. He did not seem to finish anytime soon. Again he said "il y'a un monde dans ton nez" which means, "there's a world in your nostrils".

He spent about one hour and a half removing the stuff and after that he gave up. He said it seemed as though when he removed the growth, it multiplied instead. Eventually, he stopped and asked that the culture be taken to the laboratory to find out what that was. I felt like my problems had come to an end. He told me there was still more of what he had been trying to remove from my nostrils but because I was so tired and it was taking forever to finish, he had to stop. It was such a tiring day.

Cecilia and I went to the lab to pay for the analysis of the culture after which we went home. Frida was anxious to hear what happened. I told her the problem had finally been solved. We celebrated somehow. I had a much better sleep that night.

On Monday when I went to get the results of the culture from the lab, the receptionist took a long time to call me. I was finally called inside by a lady who asked if I was Christiana and I said "yes". She handed me a sealed envelope addressed to my doctor. On the way to my doctor's office I decided to open it and when I read it, it did not make any sense to me because I did not understand even a little medical terminology. I took the envelope to my doctor's colleague, who opened it and read it. I saw him remorsefully fold the paper. He did not say a word. I asked him to interpret the medical language but he would not say a thing. He asked if I could have my parents call him.

Amazingly, I was not afraid. I did not suspect anything serious. When I got home and Frida asked about the results, I told her the doctor wanted our parents to call him. That sounded weird. She called our parents who were in the United States at the time. When they talked to the doctor, he told them I had been diagnosed with "nasopharyngeal carcinoma", a medical term for cancer of the nose which had spread to my brain. He advised them to make arrangements for me to travel to the United States for treatment since Cameroon was technologically lacking in that area of treatment.

One morning, I heard Frida scream on the phone. It sounded very much like she received bad news. I asked her what was wrong, but she would not tell me. She told me to get into the shower and so we could go and meet my doctor. My sister Vivian said, "Christie, whatever they say it is, you are healed in Jesus' name!"

Cecilia and I went to my doctor's office for the full interpretation of the diagnosis. When we arrived, I was asked to stay outside for a few minutes. I thought, if this is about me why would they discuss it with my sister and put me out? Why don't they want to tell me? I asked myself those questions but did not get upset or worried. When Cecilia came out of the office, she said "Christie, never mind, you will go to America and be treated". I did not bother to ask about what the doctor had told her. Immediately, I became consumed with the American dream.

Chapter 4

America, Home Sweet Home

Finally, my dream was coming true. I did not care about anything else, America was on the way; like my peers put it, I was going to be a "bushfaller" too. I knew everything I needed was in America. Though I still could not sleep well, I had some hope that America had the solution to my problem. I was ignorant of the fact that although good treatment was in America, what I needed most was the Healer who is everywhere.

I continued to go to school on days when I did not have a headache. I sensed that something was wrong in the house but no one told me what it was. My sister asked me to book my interview appointment at the United States Embassy in Cameroon. After making an appointment, I had to be told what was wrong with me and why I needed to travel to the United States since I was the one who would be interviewed. My sisters thought if they told me, it would make me worry and cry a lot then die, yet they had no choice but to tell me.

On a certain evening, Cecilia told me we had been invited to Pastor Angela's residence. When we got there, the Pastor asked me the question, "Christie, what would be your response if asked to give the reason for your visit to the United States?" I said I would tell the interviewer that I had a difficult health issue with my nose which could not be handled in Cameroon. She said, "No, you would have to say that your doctor's report shows that you have cancer of the nose and that you cannot be properly treated here".

After that, she said, "That is what the doctors says, but we have to believe what the Bible tells us and so the bottom line is you are healed in Jesus' name".

I was caught between if I was really sick or not, but my Pastor would not make up that lie for me, would she? I did not know what cancer was and that really did not bother me as long as she said I was healed. I wanted to go to America. That was my focal point and I knew every disease could be cured in America. Pastor Angela prayed for us and we left. Cecilia kept telling me I was healed. I did not sense their fear because my mind was entirely focused on the trip.

Chapter 5
"Pharaoh" Let Me Go!

When I went to the Embassy for my interview, I was certain my visa would be granted. I met one of my classmates there and we prayed together, but she was denied a visa. When it was my turn to be interviewed, I was asked every question and my responses seemed so pleasing. However, on the last document, which was a bank statement, the interviewer said I could not afford cancer treatment. He asked me to swell up the account and get the estimate of the treatments from America. He gave me a second chance.

I went back to the Embassy with an added bank statement, still this man asked me again and again (on six occasions) to swell up the bank account. The sixth time, he said, "No matter how much you put in this account, even if its billions, you cannot afford the treatment". I was denied the visa and left the embassy in great frustration. Right then I lost my appetite, my eyes were teary and I had a melancholic countenance.

When she came home, Cecilia saw me lying on the bed with my eyes closed but I was not sleeping. My eyes were sunken from crying. I had looked up the word cancer in the oxford dictionary which defined cancer as a growth. I found a magazine and saw a lady on one of the pages whose friends had traveled from Nigeria to London to tell her good-bye as she slowly died of cancer. I was no longer traveling to America and I now had some knowledge about what cancer was. As soon as I found out that cancer was a terminal disease, I felt even worse. My head ached more than ever. I could not sleep as I tossed on the bed. I was losing my appetite more and more, and since I really was not eating enough like I needed to, I was rapidly losing weight.

It was a good thing the diagnosis was hidden from me before. "Too much knowledge brings sorrow" (Ecclesiastes 1:18). What my sisters had been hiding from me was now known. I started having more severe headaches than ever before. Without exaggerating, they felt like intervals of electric shocks in my brain. I sat on the couch with my hands on my head as though the whole world was on top of me. No matter how well I reclined on the couch, I never got enough comfort.

I tried to go to school but I really could not attend most classes anymore. Not too long after, the students and teachers began to notice that I was sick and could not make it every day to class. One day as I got to class, the pain in my head just started pounding and tears were flowing down my face.

A classmate, Grace, suggested we go get some medication that she knew about that could calm down my pain. I had already taken multiple unhelpful medications, yet because I was so desperately in need of relief, we went and got the medication she talked about. When I took it, it didn't help either.

One cannot run away from problems and God does not allow troubles to come your way without giving you the ability to deal with them. Satan was so sure that Job could not endure the trial set before him. When people think they cannot make it through a situation, God always proves He is strong in time of weakness.

Chapter 6
Sorry, I Cannot Help You

I went to my doctor's office again so he could prescribe more effective medications to relieve the excruciating pain. When he saw me in his office, he cried out in alarm, asking, "What was I still doing in Cameroon?" I told him I was denied the visa. He confessed there was no medication that would do any better; more so, he knew the previous medications he had prescribed would not help. He felt so sorry for me and could only imagine the pain I was going through. I just wanted more medication so he went through my file and prescribed something a little different. I began to secretly take overdoses of every medication, but it still did not help. I got up every morning in a sort of dead beat.

My sister Mado came from Italy to visit me. She could not fully comprehend the situation from afar so she wanted to see how I was and how we were handling the situation psychologically. She began suggesting that she and my brother could come up with invitation documents for me to come and receive treatment in Italy.

During one of his visits, my father's doctor questioned why his blood pressure was so high. My father explained to her it was so high because he worried about my helpless state. Right away she contacted one of her colleagues in Belgium. After a long conversation, the Belgian doctor agreed to accept me as his patient. He was waiting for me to arrive but I was not going to get there in a day. It was going to be another process; besides, who was going to take care of me in Belgium? Cancer patients need a lot of assistance, encouragement and prayers; more than what the doctors and nurses can offer. Most often that support comes from loved ones in the family or angelic friends, rather than from strangers. In America, I had more relatives. It looked like that was the best place for me to go, but how was I going to get there?

One day, I got up in the middle of the night after tossing and turning in bed several times. I was about to wake Frida and Cecilia up from sleep to pray a last prayer over me because I was convinced I would die that night. I wished ice would help, but it did not. The pain was intolerable. I contemplated and settled on bearing the excruciating pain alone. I was restless, so I went to the restroom and just cried. As I sobbed, I placed my hands on every side of my head. I tried in every way not to make myself heard. Since I could not cry freely, I felt like the pain was stuffed down my throat. I said "God please give me just a little minute of sleep", sprinkling water on my head. I left the restroom and went back to bed where I continued to toss left and right and change the position of my pillow. By the time Mado had returned to Italy my eyes became red in color and puffy. One morning, I went to the mirror and noticed my eyes were crossed.

Pastor Angela kept praying for me. Like never before I knew my name was on the obituary list. I started confessing my sins. Every day I waited until my sisters went to work, and then I would cry out to God. Crying was part of my daily routine. I could not say a prayer without crying and I did not even know what to tell God. I asked God if He could not see me and feel my pain. I made vows by telling God if only He took me to America, I would give a financial gift of an incredible amount for the work of the kingdom. Did God need that to get me where I wanted? Absolutely not!

Later when my condition worsened, I realized I was not asking God for the right thing. I was asking Him more to grant my request to go to America. I began to pray, God please heal me right where I am. I do not need to go to America if that is not your plan for me. Sometimes it sounds like it is so easy to know what to ask God, but there are things God does not want us to ignore.

I realized that I needed to have more purpose to life than just desiring a wish. Though I had been in pain, my "joie de vivre" (fear of God) was half hearted, especially when I thought of going to America. Nevertheless, these disappointments completely killed all my vivacity. In II Chronicles 16:12, "Asa was afflicted with a disease in his feet. Though his disease was severe, even in his illness he did not seek help from the Lord, but only from physicians. Then in the forty-first year of his reign, Asa died and rested with his fathers. "

It was at this point I desired the Lord more than physicians. Though I had been calling on the Lord, I wanted His healing power more than Him. Through one of Pastor Benny Hinn's teachings he explained that people cannot want to receive healing and reject the Healer. In other words, he was explaining that one should receive Jesus Christ as the Lord and Savior who heals all manner of diseases. That ministered to me. It described the old me who just sought the Lord's hand and not His face. I thought my destiny was in the hands of the man who denied me the visa to America. I was convinced that the more he denied me the visa, the closer I was drawn to death. Ironically, the more he denied me the visa, the more I died in the flesh and hungered for more of Jesus.

Many ask for what they want and not what they need. At the time I needed to be healed, but I asked God more for the opportunity to go to America rather than getting healed. We may think we know how to make our requests known to God but it is wise to check our priorities. Like a good father who is able to afford his daughter's new shoes and school requirements, it will be wiser for him to see that she has her school items, which is a need, before her new pair of shoes, which is a want. God too is an organized God.

He wants His children to prioritize too. Do you still doubt this fact? It is written: "Seek ye first the kingdom of God and His righteousness, and all these things shall be added unto you" (Matthew 6:33). Here, righteousness is God's first priority. Nowadays priorities differ, but above all, righteousness must take precedence.

Not too long after, my sister Patricia and her husband Raymond were informed that my situation was getting worse. They began putting together the necessary documents for me to request an American visa again. My interviewer was still the same man who had denied me previously. Again, he said I should present a cost estimate of the treatment and get a bank statement that matched the estimate. I presented the estimate and the bank statement as he requested. He said the treatment was going to be extensive, and because I had just one doctor's estimate with an accompanied bank statement, he said he needed to see all the other doctors' estimates and more bank statements.

When Patricia met other doctors, they wrote letters to the Embassy saying they could not come up with their estimates until they reexamined me and saw how far the cancer had spread. Only then would they be able to figure out how much treatment I needed and how much I was going to be billed.

The interviewer made me come to the embassy again about six times, after which he denied me a visa repeatedly. I thought there were demons in him. I did not care at this time about trying to convince him so I insulted him and told him how inhumane he was. He got up from his seat and moved to the back to grab a cup of coffee. I had borne enough grief and I thought he was very wicked to have denied a visa to someone like me who needed a chance to live.

It had been a year since I was diagnosed with cancer, which was malignant (potentially fatal). As I left the Embassy on my way to the house, I was soliloquizing and sniveling within. I lay on my bed and began to weep. As I looked at the sky through the window pane I felt as though the world's misery had come upon me.

Thereafter, I began to grumble and talk back to God. "Lord, why have you done this to me? Why, why, why do you grant the visa to those who don't serve you and yet reward your servant in such a shameful way? People who don't care about you are drinking and getting drunk day and night and they have good sleep at night and here am I trying to stay in your presence. Why haven't you considered my plea? People who serve false gods such as 'olomba olomba' and 'bahaola' are getting visas. Why not grant me the visa, me who has surrendered worldly pleasures? Why didn't you respond to my plea Lord? Why, why, why?" The truth I did not understand then was that God has three responses to every plea, which are: Yes, No or Wait. These responses do not determine His sovereignty. He is sovereign irrespective of how He responds.

Chapter 7
How Will Urine Therapy Cure Cancer?

One morning, I got up feeling unusual. I looked in the mirror and noticed my eyes were crossed and my vision was blurred. As my eyesight grew worse, I could not stand the glow of sunlight and the radiance of the television rays. My hand had to be held by someone in order for me to walk in the right direction. Claudia, my niece, held my hand and helped me walk to places I wanted to go. I had to wear sunshades to block the rays of the sun from coming directly into my eyes. I was later declared legally blind.

At this point I decided it was time to try one of my classmate's ideas, who had told me about a strange cure she had read about some time ago. It was called "urine therapy". She said it could cure every disease on planet earth. She said one had to drink his own early morning urine every day. I was in serious pain and desperately needed a little bit of sleep, which I still could not get. I started to collect and drink my urine in the mornings together with overdoses of multitudes of medications, none of which helped me at all.

One day Cecilia's friend told her that urine therapy was not a holy practice. Furthermore, she explained that it did not make any sense for me to drink what God had created to be eliminated from our body system. How does science explain the use of recycled urine in the body? Was it biblical? No! So I stopped drinking my urine. I changed my diet and began eating healthy foods but nothing changed.

One evening Brother Bruno, a brother I met at the University of Yaounde campus fellowship, came to check on me. I started telling him how God had given people who did not serve Him good health instead of people like me who adored Him. He narrated the story of the children of Israel who spent longer years in their journey because of murmuring and complaining and advised me to stop complaining. It must have been the Holy Ghost who convicted me through his witnessing because right away I repented. He advised me to praise God more. Thereafter I began to praise God even though my situation did not look like it was changing.

The enemy did all he could to have me accept his ugly lies. In the mornings as I started praying, I began to see myself in a casket. I saw how my siblings cried around my grave. I saw how my casket was descending in the ground. I did not share this with anyone. When I knelt down to pray, I saw myself in the casket. I said in my prayers, "Lord, if it is your will for me to die, I accept death in exchange for this pain".

The enemy wanted me to accept death and the coffin he had for me. I have heard people narrate stories of how they bought their own coffins or caskets because they received a bad medical report. I had accepted death and wanted to die but I worried about the way my siblings would handle it. Some Christians, when faced with a terminal disease, claim to have faith in God yet begin making preparations for their funerals. However, when situations look irreparable and unchanging, it does not necessarily mean that one will die.

Death should not be a scary part of destiny, because it will happen to all of us some day. Not everyone gives up when faced with a tough situation. For example, take a look at Job's life (Job 1-2), the woman with the issue of blood (Matthew 9:18-25), or worse still, Lazarus who died and was buried (John 11:38-44). A lot of us would have spoken just like Mary Magdalene who thought that Jesus came too late and could only perform a miracle before her brother's death. Though Jesus wept, His mind was conditioned to wake Lazarus from the dead. Why would Jesus weep for a situation He could easily solve?

Jesus is compassionate and knows what pain and suffering feels like. He feels what we feel just like He felt the pain of loss that Mary Magdalene experienced. It is hard to watch your sister or brother cry and not cry with them. I have cried sometimes just because I saw other people cry. If Jesus lacked faith he would not have called Lazarus out from the tomb. His faith matched his actions. We may cry sometimes but that does not mean we lack trust in God. God is never unfaithful, He is always on time. The morning always comes and the sun always returns, and that portrays God's faithfulness.

Sometimes people shift from having great faith to very little faith, like I did. Some people have great faith when faced with problems they think can be solved easily. On the other hand, others have great faith when faced with greater challenges. My faith began to decrease as my health grew worse and even then my confessions did not match the little faith I did possess. At this time, my faith was supposed to match what I was saying and hoping through prayer. Irrespective of the casket in which I saw myself, I was supposed to believe I would not die. I trusted

God to heal me but was distracted by the casket vision, resigning myself to die.

My prayers changed to: "Dear Lord, I know that you are my only Lord and Savior, in spite of all these things that are happening to me. Please forgive all my transgressions. I choose to forgive even those I hate. I choose to let go of my playful and deceptive past. If there be any unconfessed sins that I am unaware of please forgive me. Forgive me for every ungodly relationship I was ever involved in. Forgive me for ever being lukewarm about you. There is nothing that I do right before you, even as I pray. Please forgive me. Holy Ghost please intercede for me because the Bible says you pray for me when I do not know how to pray. I don't want to suffer on earth and then suffer again in hell. Please accept me in the kingdom of heaven when I die". I had accepted death but did not know when it was going to happen. I continued to see myself in the casket with my siblings crying around it.

One day I was talking to Brother Bruno again and happened to describe the imagery of myself in the casket. Right away, he said that was from the devil. He told me if I saw that image again, I should say cancer will die in my place in Jesus' name! He explained that life and death were in the power of the tongue.

When the image surfaced again, like an expert warrior I loudly declared "Cancer will die in my place in Jesus' name!" I began to see the power of the tongue as it is written in Proverbs 18:21, "Life and death are in the power of the tongue and those who love it will eat its fruits". Slowly but surely, I began to see a long roll of paper on which was written "cancer" which replaced me in the casket. I rejoiced whenever I saw this. Though the pain was not gone, I bore in mind that I only owed God praise.

My church (Abundant Life Faith Chapel International) was preparing to receive a visiting Prophet of God, Prince Zilly Agrey from Nigeria. At that time I wanted to do everything the word of God said in order to tap into my blessing. I knew his ministry was another fertile ground in which I could sow my seed. I thought I could participate by making flyers and buying the welcome flowers for the little flower girl, Golda, who would present them to the man of God. I thought if I gave to the man of God, God would also bless me by answering my request. I was not well versed in the scriptures and was not even aware of Matthew 10:41-42: "If you give to a prophet of God even a cup of water because he is my servant, you will receive a prophet's reward". I called Pastor Angela and asked her if I could go ahead and gather a team of saints to help with my vision and she granted my request. It was beautifully accomplished.

It was December again and once more Christmas was around the corner. People were getting ready to celebrate but nothing seemed to be happening in my world. My younger brother Ako knew that I was sick but did not know why. He began to ask Frida why I was so pale and why I had lost my appetite. Frida told him that I had cancer. He expressed deep remorse and asked me to take some pictures. We had not taken pictures together for ages so I accepted.

On one afternoon, I sat on the bed with sunken cheeks and when Frida saw me she noticed I had been crying. She did not want me crying all the time. She did not want me thinking I was going to die so she said, "Christie, stop thinking that you have a helpless situation. Do you want us to go to the hospital just so you can see that some people are in a worse situation than you? Know that yours is nothing compared to them". I did not catch her trick until one day while she sat in the living room alone, I saw her; not even with a tissue, but with a face towel, wiping her tears. She was silently weeping. As soon as I stepped in the living room, she went to another room. I began to understand how she too was being affected.

On Christmas day, I lay on the bed and because my head ached dreadfully, I stayed at home. Cecilia asked if I wanted to go out with Ako. My response was an obvious "No". She wanted me to just get out of the house a little bit. My four friends were all out of town. Finally, I went with Ako to visit our cousin Elvis. I did not regret going out because we had fun and I had some distraction from my pain. We talked a lot about America and how we would go there someday. I felt like I had activated that "America dream" again.

Days passed and preparation began again for another visiting man of God, Pastor Olubi Johnson from Nigeria. The congregation was on a fast. I did not think I should participate because I was so sick, but a more dedicated church member, Sister Phina, advised me to fast because I needed to be healed. This time I knew why I was fasting and had been told that if I thought I could not, I should break it. It was amazing how I had no appetite before but when I committed my mind to fast, I was suddenly hungry and wanted to eat. I finally made it from morning until 10:00pm when we were supposed to break the fast. My head ached more than ever before. Sister Phina told me the enemy did not want me to be healed and that was why I had those terrible headaches. At the time we all wanted to punch this enemy so we associated every discomfort in relation to him.

I received the baptism of the Holy Ghost during that night vigil under Pastor Olubi's ministering. While he preached, I felt like my neck could not support my head any longer to the point that I leaned on the shoulder of an unknown lady who sat by me. She saw me struggling and how the tears were constantly flowing down my cheeks. I overheard a visitor ask a member of the church why I was crying and they replied "She is crying because she is sick". At first I did not cry because my head ached, but tears were flowing involuntarily down my face as the pastor preached.

When I got home I did not know what to do with such pain. I wished I had some valium pills to take so I could sleep. The one thing I remember so vividly was that I had some soda after my fast. Later, I was told that was the worst thing to do. I was congratulated by a church member for fasting that long, but what about the headaches? When were they going to stop? I began asking myself, did I really need to fast in such a state? Would God have me fast in that state for those long hours? No!

On a certain Tuesday during Bible study, I told Frida that I could feel the pain again far above its normal beat. She asked if I wanted to leave but I refused because the pastor was rounding up. As soon as the pastor said the closing prayer, we hurried home as though some relieving medications were there for me.

After church service on Sunday I left in tears. I was not embarrassed at how I cried because no one felt what I was feeling. A sister in Christ came by to find out why I was crying and when I told her I had a headache she said, "Why do you have a headache when you are a child of God? Speak the word of God and it will leave."

I did not find that funny. Why had she not prayed for me? She was so ignorant of what was going on with me but still I did not find her advice a good approach. I thought she was so unfriendly. I began to understand that not everyone in the church knew how to exercise their faith when they met someone in crisis. Sometimes, people's level of faith can cause others to think they do not believe at all. I would think that when one sees a believer who is sick, one should extend an invitation to pray rather than say they ought not to be sick. To say that Christians should not be sick is not true; as long as this flesh lives in this world, it will undergo changes and responses to environments, weather, food, health choices, peace in the place of conflict, prayer instead of discouragement, etc.

On the other hand, read what another sister in the church wrote when I told her I had a headache; this was encouraging.

> 11-01-03
>
> my dear christy,
>
> I love You. Don't bother about what the devil is telling you in your body. Even this year you shall blossom in your health.
>
> Tell yourself that you are well.
>
> I will visit you, don't know when.
>
> Victors don't cry, they sing. You are victorious. You are well shout Hallelujah.
>
> Be strong.
>
> You can see well. Forget everything & be strong.
>
> Psa 27. Love Crysta.

Crystabelle, another saint in the church prayed for me and wrote this little healing note.

Note from the kind-hearted lady in Nevada who paid for my ticket.

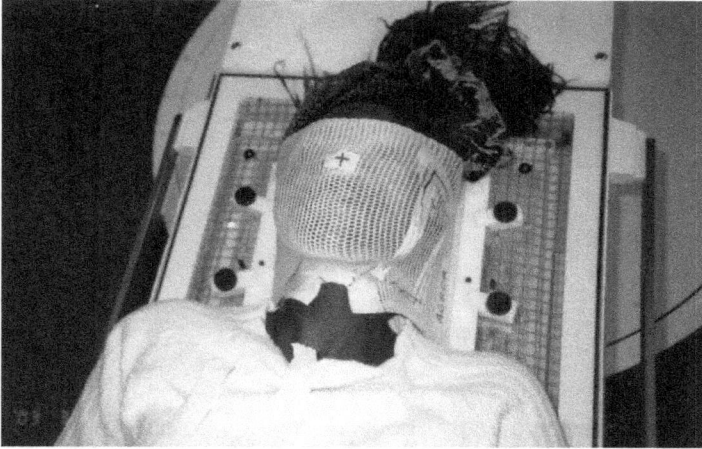

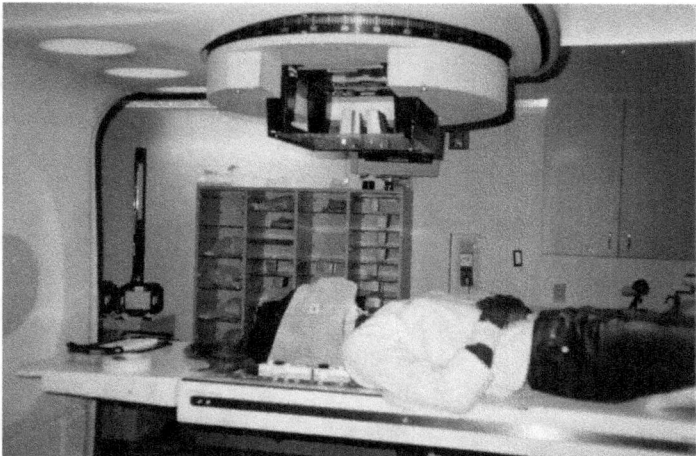

Radiation treatments in the hospital.

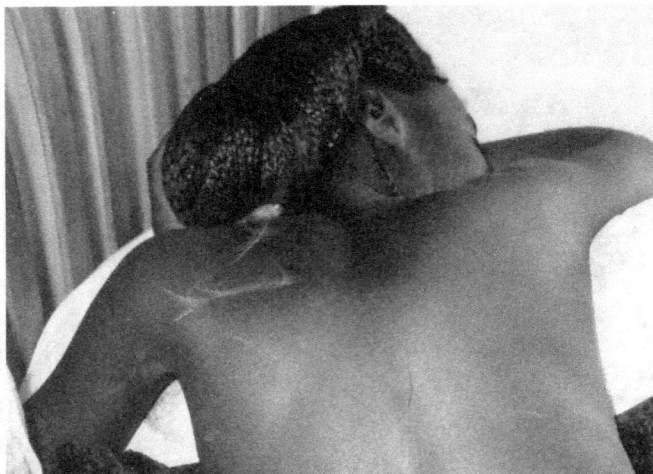

Radiation therapy effects on my jaw, neck and back.
(It looked like flaking charcoal).

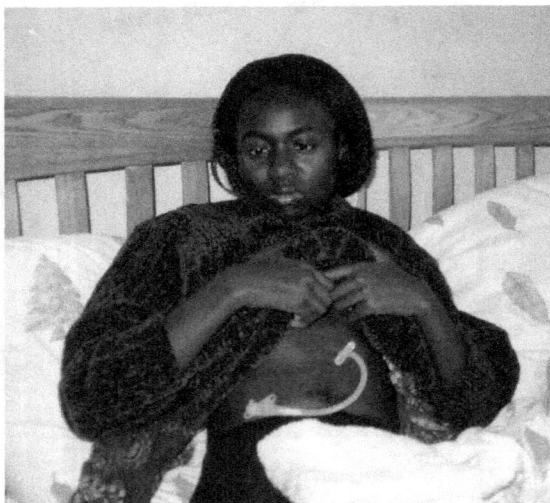

The feeding tube I had for six months.

Smiling in the beauty of complete healing.

An oncologist called Patricia and my parents to tell them that it would be best to stop trying to get me into the United States because the report showed the cancer had spread extensively. Since it had been over a year since my diagnosis, he thought it would have been better for them to save their money instead of bringing me to America then wasting more money to ship my corpse back to Cameroon. That was a clear message that my chances of living were close to zero. He was speaking from a scientific perspective. Patricia did not accept the fact that I could die. She believed that I would get better after the treatments.

I often listened to Reverend Umah Ukpai's healing messages and I laughed a lot as he expressed how people were healed of terrible diseases through the power of God and how God's power superseded scientific knowledge. I felt like I really did not know how to pray as I meditated on healing scriptures and Psalms. I had a book, "Prayer Rain" by Dr. DK Olukoya, which contained healing prayers based on the word of God which strengthened my faith.

Surprisingly, one Sunday, I saw a relative I had not seen in ages. We were so happy to see each other. She introduced me to her fiancé who was also a born again Christian. After church service, we talked about the past and the people we knew and where they were, but she could see a big change in me. She intuitively sensed that something was not right. Out of curiosity she began to ask why I looked that way and I told her that I was sick. She said, "I know that God is able to heal all kinds of diseases except two that I've never seen Him heal, which are AIDS and cancer". I told her I was diagnosed with cancer of the nose and the brain after which she said, "It is well, my fiancé and I will pray for you". I did not succumb to her unbelief and pondered what she was going to pray about and also to whom she would pray since she had never seen God heal cancer.

Nevertheless, out of desperation, I let them pray for me. This relative of mine was a fluent holy tongue speaker and she could quote many scriptures so I thought she was an expert in the word. However, I began to see that there were some immature believers of the word of God, and because they did not see, they did not believe.

On the other hand it is written, "It is impossible to please God without faith" (Heb 11:6). In other words, faith believes in the promises of God about the outcome of whatever circumstance one is facing; regardless of how intense it may look, feel or seems impossible by man's reasoning.

Faith does not focus on the present; it invites and grabs the future into the present. The scripture in Hebrews 11:1 commences with "Now...", meaning although science portrayed evidence of cancer, regardless of the headaches or how my eyes were crossed, at that very moment I had to accept that I was already healed. I had to see it and confess it too.

How could I see it? Faith does not view the possibility of getting healed, it looks through the eyes of the healer who is God and confirms that it is already done. The word of God is not in the process of becoming established. It is already confirmed and will remain that way. Hope in the Healer is not an assuming expression. In other words, it would not be right for me to say I am sick and maybe God will heal me, because God never waits to perform His word. The scripture says, He watches over His word to perform it (Jeremiah 1:12), meaning He watches over what He has already done. He watches over the price that was paid through His son Jesus. It is an assurance and not a probability. Most pregnant women shop for their babies prior to delivery because they have faith the baby will be born alive. Who told them so? Is it the case with every woman? No, but by faith it happens most of the time. It is an unrecognized faith. If it were a matter of assumption, they would wait until after the birth to shop for their baby. God makes sure that whenever His word is backed by our action, His will for our lives is brought to manifestation.

Jeremiah 33:3 says, "Call on me and I will answer you and I will show you great and mighty things which thou knowest not". If I had died, would it mean that God did not watch His word to perform it? No. If I had died, could I be brought back to life in Jesus' name? Yes. The Bible referred to Jairus' daughter as a sleeping child. When Jesus told the sinner on the cross that he would be with Him in paradise, that man was not going to appear in paradise still hanging on the cross. In other words, I would have died in the flesh yet been healed in the presence of the Lord.

I surrendered my desires of going to America and began seeing myself healed according to God's word. Crying to myself did not seem to help, it was a partial expression of my pain that always left me in a state of self pity, anguish and loss of appetite. Crying to God made a difference because afterward, I had hope that He had seen and heard me and something good would come out of it.

"Record my lament; list my tears on your scroll. Are they not in your record?" Psalm 56:8 (NIV).

It's alright to cry in painful situations but do not let the pain overwhelm your belief in God's word. When we allow our tears and pain to overrule our trust in God, that's when we start murmuring and complaining and nothing good will come out it. That is exactly what happened to the children of Israel. God allowed them to walk through the wilderness for 40 years instead of the 11 days it should have taken them to cross over.

In January, Patricia and Raymond put more documents together for me to request a visa again. This time we thought we needed power from above for my visa to be granted. A top government official, Embassy doctors and a senator wrote letters of appeal to the interviewer asking for my visa to be granted so I could have a chance to live. God did not allow the interviewer to grant me the visa yet again. I was so assured in my spirit that once the interviewer saw the letters of appeal from those dignitaries, he would reverse his decision. God did not want me to put my trust in man or in the power of a man's office. God wanted me to recognize that He was in control and no one else had the power to rewind, fast forward or wipe out His plan for me. He made sure that no one else could get the glory out of what He had done.

The refusal this time literally meant that the power of the aforementioned officials was not strong enough to direct or impose the mind of the interviewer to grant my visa. God alone has that power. "The king's heart is in the hand of the Lord; He directs it like a watercourse wherever He pleases" Proverbs 21:1 (NIV). We thought it was wise to use high ranking personnel, but with God, there is none beside Him.

God told Moses in the book of Exodus that He was going to harden the heart of Pharaoh. Even after signs and wonders were manifested with plagues of blood, frogs, flies, boils, hail, gnats and locust, Pharaoh still did not let the children of Israel go. The Lord allowed the heart of Pharaoh to become hardened because He wanted everyone to know that He alone is LORD.

Perhaps the interviewer's heart was hardened because God wanted me and others to know that He is the LORD. Exodus 10:1-2 says, "Then the Lord said to Moses, Go to Pharaoh, for I have hardened his heart and the hearts of his officials so that I may perform these miraculous signs of mine among them that you may tell your children and grandchildren how I dealt harshly with the Egyptians and how I performed my signs among them, and that you may know that I am the Lord" (NIV). If I had been granted the visa at that time, I would have attributed the success to the official's intervention. Thank God He did not allow it to be so.

Frida and I went to seek help at a hospital where the doctors managed to administer radiation in their limited capacity. My doctor had advised me to receive treatment in my country only as a last resort. The doctors in Cameroon did not have all the needed requirements nor had they familiarized themselves enough with that treatment. My doctor predicted it was highly risky for such an advanced stage of cancer to be handled in my country. He overtly expressed his fear of me dying in the hands of a doctor who had limited resources to help. He stood firm that since I had the means of traveling, I should settle for nothing else.

I understood his fears, but what about my pain? Frida asked if I wanted to try the treatment in my country. Without telling my doctors and without my parents' approval or opinion, I chose to get the treatment in Cameroon regardless of the limitations. We went to see the doctor in charge of cancer treatment at the hospital and when we arrived, we were told he was traveling and would only come back on a certain Thursday. I so badly needed the treatment, but how was I going to get it without the approval of my initial doctor?

I agreed to get the treatment anyway. One could evidently see the need on my face. The Thursday of my doctor's appointment happened to be the day of my next and last appointment with the American Embassy. Was this a coincidence? No it was not. Since my interview was scheduled to be in the morning, if they denied me again, this time I would go straight ahead and begin the unpromising treatment my doctor had warned against. Though I was calling on God for help, at this point, I felt that God was sleeping on my case. Despite my feelings, that was not true. It is written in Psalm 121:4, "Indeed, he who watches over Israel will neither slumber nor sleep."

A few days before the interview, I had a dream in which I was in a roundabout building made of gold. A lion was sitting at the front. I touched the lion's mouth and the lion did not roar neither did it harm me. It was a very peaceful lion and I could lay my hands on it without fear. So what did this mean? Jesus is the Lion of the tribe of Judah and His peace surpasses all human understanding. In the natural, lions are called the king of the jungle but this lion was the only animal in this golden building. In my human reasoning I would think if one came in contact with a lion, it would tear him apart then eat him. What did this dream mean?

I asked the Holy Spirit and He ministered to me that the Lord was going to take me to a land I had never seen. In this land all would be new in my eyes. I would not die from sickness or situations that human beings fear most because He is able to demystify the unknown. He was the one in control of the situation and would lead me safely. As long as we remained friends, He would do what man thinks is impossible. He would show me His gentleness, kindness and favor and I would finally get to the place that had been so difficult for me to reach, like the miners who dig deep for gold. He was showing me that He already scheduled me to be there. The entire message was summed up to be, "Fear not for I am with you even to the ends of the earth." That was the meaning of the dream.

On the day before the last interview, I was not excited about anything and Cecilia asked me to call Pastor Angela and request a word from her. I called and told her I had another appointment at the Embassy the next day. I said, "Pastor, say a word". She said, "When you get there, they will hesitate to give you the visa but they will grant it to you this time." All along we had been praying and believing in God for my visa but her speech had never been this detailed and specific. Were the words of the prophetess true?

On January 16th 2003, we got up with worship songs stirring the atmosphere of the house. I read Psalm

138 and said a prayer for healing from a Christian prayer book entitled "Prayer Rain" by Dr. D.K. Olukoya. I also anointed myself and we agreed in prayer with my two sisters, cousin and niece. Matthew 18:18-20 says, "I tell you the truth, whatever you bind on earth will be bound in heaven, and whatever you loose on earth will be loosed in heaven. Again, I tell you that if two of you on earth agree about anything you ask for, it will be done for you by my Father in heaven. Where two or three come together in my name, there am I with them."

On our way to the Embassy, I told my cousin Emilienne if I was granted that visa, it was because God made it possible and not because of the documents I had with me, and she said "Amen" to that. Only those who are to be interviewed could get into the Embassy so Emilienne was outside waiting for me. When the time came for me to plead my case, the interviewer asked for every document I had.

She took a glance at them and later asked, "Who is Grace?" This question came up as she saw a letter sent from Patricia's church, Grace Tabernacle. I replied, "Grace is not someone, it is the church my sister attends in the United States." She took all my documents and went to one of her colleagues and they whispered to one another while I was waiting, just like my pastor had told me. The interviewer came back and said, "Congratulations, you have been approved to have the American visa. Go ahead and pay your issuance fee." I really was not excited but I could feel my spirit whisper, Alas! It was too evident that this was the Lord's doing.

After paying the fee, I needed to come back at 4:00pm to get my passport with my visa in it. I stepped out and looked around for Emilienne but she had gone for a little walk to the bakery. The Lord had not allowed anyone else to be around so we could fully recognize that it was His doing. I called Frida and told her the good news. She was so excited and screamed joyously. The expression of her emotion was not at all questionable. Proverbs 14:10 says, "Each heart knows its own bitterness and no one else can share its joy."

Emilienne came back to check on me and I told her the good news. We went to a surrounding neighborhood to visit a family friend, after which we came back at 4:00pm to get my visa. Later on, we went home and Cecilia wanted to hear all about the interview. It was miracle service night at church and it was going to be my last attendance so I did not miss it. Emilienne came along with me and the service seemed to end too soon. Thereafter, I told Pastor Chris and Pastor Angela that everything happened just like the Lord had shown her. She gave me a hug and said, "God is good!"

Chapter 8
Rejoice, but Know the Battle is Not Over Yet

My flight was scheduled for the next Thursday and I had to pick up my ticket. When Frida and I went to get my ticket from the Air France Agency, one of the representatives looked at me and said, "I hope it's not the girl at the back who is scheduled to travel." Frida responded, "She is the one traveling." He told her that he was not going to give me the ticket because I looked like I was at a dying stage and he did not believe I would make it to the United States on their flight. He explained my appearance was a high risk and suggested I see the Air France doctor to receive a permission note, without which I could not travel.

Frida and I consulted the French doctor, whom after examining my nostrils started asking questions such as, "How old are you?" I said, "I am twenty-three years old." He folded his arms and looked at me then said, "You deserve a chance to live and need to reach America as soon as possible, so I wish you good luck in your treatment." He asked for my doctor's number, which we gave him. He called my doctor and instructed him to tell me to take in a deep breath when the plane was taking off and landing because he feared my breathing pattern could stop, leaving me gasping for air when the plane ascended or descended. He wrote a note asking the airline representative to hand over my ticket.

On January 20th 2003, I went to get my ticket. I had to travel on Thursday. According to the payment agreement, if I missed traveling on Thursday, the ticket would not have been useful. It was non-refundable and could not be exchanged. This ticket was a gift from a lady in America who later became a family friend. My mother had only mentioned that her daughter was diagnosed with cancer and would be coming to the United States by God's grace. She felt so touched by the fact that I was only 23 years old that she handed Patricia an envelope with a check enclosed to pay for the ticket.

On Wednesday, some Christian fellowship friends, Brother Bruno, Jude, Tabi, Miatta and Miriam, came to pray for me, iron my clothes and chat. I did not know what was in my luggage; my sisters did the packing for me. On Thursday morning, Frida and I made our last visit to my doctor's office. He told me about the breathing exercise I had to do on the plane and wished me a good recovery.

About 5:00pm, we headed to the airport where an officer said I could not travel with an electronic ticket. They did some verification shortly after which I was told I could travel. It was clear to me at this point that everywhere I made a stop, there was someone who tried to prevent me from moving ahead but the God who granted me the visa was in the business of perfecting that which He had started. When God blesses, the enemy still looks for avenues to steal, kill or destroy, but this time God did not let him have his way. It seemed like the enemy monitored everywhere I went but God was with me.

When Pharaoh finally let the children of Israel leave Egypt, he probably thought later on that he had blundered. He may have thought the power to say yes or no was totally in his ability, but God's will superseded. The enemy may follow closely behind after God opens the way for us to be blessed, just like Pharaoh's soldiers who followed the children of Israel towards the Red Sea. However, when one wins a battle it does not mean prayer time is over. That is why God wants His children to pray without ceasing, because the enemy is not sleeping. He is walking to and fro in the earth, seeking whom he may devour. When Jesus asked His disciples to pray, He left them and shortly thereafter found they had all fallen asleep. Sometimes we get tired and may not pray as we should, but God's grace and mercy speaks for us.

Cecilia escorted me to my last stop and said a prayer on my behalf. When she left, I looked around to see who the Holy Spirit was going to put me in connection with, so I could carry on a conversation. I waited until saw a boy who looked similar to someone I saw at the Embassy. He had a friend with him and they sat close to me. When he said I looked familiar, we introduced ourselves and started conversing, disclosing our destinations in the United States. His name was Joe and his friend's name was Gregory. Once inside the plane, my seat was next to a Chinese man whose brother sat on the same row as Gregory. They agreed to exchange seats and Gregory sat next to me. Six hours later, we arrived at Charles de Gaulle Airport in Paris where Joe and Gregory helped me locate my next destination since I could not see nor hear well. We separated at Terminal 1. As I made my way towards Terminal 2, it occurred to me that Joe and Gregory were what I term "human angels" whom God had allowed to help me.

When I alighted the mini bus and arrived at the other end of Terminal 2, I started looking for the United

Airlines stand. I tried to make my way by asking a security officer where the stand was and all he did was stretch his hand towards a direction. That was mean enough to get me going. Then I met a French couple and asked them the same question and they happened to be going that way so they asked me to follow them. Thank God for another set of angels. When we got close to the Agency's stand, they pointed out the stand I was looking for and I thanked them, after which they continued their walk.

I arrived at the stand and got my continuation tickets. The Agency's security guard was a very beautiful light skinned lady named Annick. When she looked at my passport, she said, "Wow, you come from Cameroon. Nice to see you, I am a Cameroonian too. Your visa is a medical visa. I wonder how you got that, you are special!" I asked her why she said so and she told me about her brother who was sick and had tried to get the same medical visa to no avail. She said her brother finally got the visa when he presented that he simply wanted to go visit the United States for leisure.

She asked if it was okay for her to find out what the problem was and I told her I had been diagnosed with an advanced stage of cancer. She said I was too young to have been diagnosed with such a disease. I told her about the arrangement my brother Sampson made to see me in Paris and she gave me her phone so I could call him. I dialed his number and he expressed his excitement. I told him it was Annick's phone and asked him to say hello and express his gratitude for allowing me the use of her phone. She told him in which area of the airport I was located. Annick handed the phone back to me but we agreed not to talk on her phone any further.

90

Later, he called back explaining he was not allowed to come and see me because I did not have a transit visa. That sounded funny. Annick tried to talk to the colleagues on the other side to let him see me but they explained why they could not. She asked if they could only get the things my brother had brought and send them to me on her behalf, which they did. I continued my conversation with my brother and he told me it was well with my situation. I also had a few things for him. Annick asked me to leave them with her as they agreed to meet and exchange the items in person.

Annick told me to sit where we could talk and she could have a proper view of me. She got me some chocolate milk, tea and cake. I did not have an appetite but managed to eat what she offered. I waited for my next plane for about eight hours. When it was time for me to go, she asked one of her colleagues to lead me onto the plane. I heartily thanked her for being so kind and got her phone number. As I was led onto the plane, I heard her say, "Bye, Christiana" and I said, "Bye-bye". As I sat in my seat, I pondered what an angel she was. Thank God for her.

While on the flight to San Francisco, California, I took a pain killer which did not help. I did not order any food nor utter any words to the person next to me. He just kept watching me as I tried to lean my head on my seat and took one medication after the other.

Before landing in the United States, the air hostess handed me a yellow paper to fill out which had to be presented at our next stop. I was tired when she gave it to me so I dropped it on the plane. When I arrived where I was supposed to present the paper, I told the lady in charge that I did not have it. She sent me to a nearby detention office, which is where international travelers are repatriated (sent to their home country) for having faulty documents. When I got there, I was interviewed in the same approach as at the Embassy: What was my name? Where was I going? Why was I going there? Who was sponsoring my trip? I was not scared of anything. Five minutes later, my luggage was brought to me. They asked to see my documents and had me fill out the same yellow paper. I left from there and went to check in my luggage and other loads. Then, I called my mom who was in Sparks, Nevada and she was so happy I had made it that far. I felt relieved that I was almost there.

I had to be carried by wheelchair from there and I could hear my name being called over the speakers. I told a lady I could hear my name but did not know where the message came from. She took me to the front desk after which I found my way to my next spot where I sat waiting for my next flight. I was asked if I still needed the wheel chair and I said no because it was almost time to check in for my last destination, Nevada.

On the plane a little girl of about three years of age was crying tremendously because she had dropped her doll somewhere she did not know. Sooner than she imagined, an officer found her doll after which, the atmosphere was calm. In an hour we landed at the Reno/Tahoe airport. As I walked through the crowd, I saw my mother, Patricia and Raymond with their three kids, plus other family and friends. Everyone gave me a hug after which they took my luggage to the car. We arrived at the house where my dad and I were so excited to see each other. After a shower, my sister and mom sorted my belongings. I ate and we talked a little then they left me alone to rest, but I left the lights on as I could not sleep.

In the morning, my cousin Queenta came by and we were excited to see each other. Brother DeSean and Sister Theresa were the first members of Grace Tabernacle I met who prayed for me. That night Aunty Pauline and my parents stayed awake all night praying for me.

On Sunday morning we went to Grace Tabernacle Church. I met Pastor Norris and First Lady Remintha DuPree and all the saints who had been interceding for me. We were so happy to meet one another.

I went to see the doctor on Monday. As she drove to the Radiology Oncologist's office Patricia tried to familiarize me with the questions the doctors might ask. When we arrived, I met Dr. Jonathan Tay who was one of my doctors. He looked through my nostrils and could obviously see the cancer cells. He began asking questions related to the kind of cancer I had. He said it was common among Asians. He asked if I had ever been to China and I said "No". He also asked if I had ever lived in an industrialized area and I remembered we lived for ages near the chocolate company, bakery and brewery companies and so I said "Yes". He said it may be a possibility but one can never really arrive at the reason why a patient has cancer.

He questioned me continually. Did I ever smoke? "No", never had I tried to. Do we eat smoked fish? "Yes", we do in some of our African dishes. Did anyone in the family ever have cancer? "No". He asked how much pain I was feeling at the time and what I was struggling with. I told him how I saw double images of the same objects and of people, and about the headaches and difficulty sleeping, etc. He explained that he wished it were not so but according to medical science, after the treatment of nasopharyngeal carcinoma, my hair might fall off and I may lose my eyesight completely. Since the cancer had already affected my optic nerves so badly he wanted to prepare my mind for such an occurrence as blindness.

He added that after the treatment, there could be a possibility of a poor functioning of my pituitary glands, change of taste, very little secretion of saliva and teeth damage. He explained after viewing my latest scan films that the cancer had spread to part of my brain. He and the other doctors suggested I take radiation treatments alongside the chemotherapy.

Chapter 9
You Don't Know How It Feels Until You Experience It

The doctors agreed that I was going to get 35 radiations and 3-loaded chemo's. I had a total of 70 injections in my belly. My best nurse Angie injected two in my belly every thirty minutes before I was radiated. Whenever I went to the radiation room, the nurses (two beautiful ladies who were both named Diana) had to put a mask on my face. It had been rightly designed to fit just my face. A cross sign was drawn on the front, which marked the specific area where the cancer cells were located. I took it to be the cross on which my troubles were nailed. Each time they put the mask on my face, it was tightly fitted and attached to the table that I laid on. I was asked to lie still. I had to be left in the room all by myself while the radiation team watched me through the outer monitor. They reminded me if I had a panic attack to raise my hand and they would come to my rescue.

Fear did not escape my mind while lying inside that dim room. Sometimes I raised my hand and almost told them I couldn't go through with the procedure. The radiation team did not understand that I was in fear. I pretended sometimes that I was thirsty or wanted to cough. They lowered the table, took the mask off my face and had me relax for a few minutes, after which they got me ready again and heightened the table I was lying on.

All I saw were the radiation machines rotating close to my face, with the red sparkling laser lights shining from every angle of the room. Underneath the mask I mumbled II Timothy 1:7, "For God has not given us a spirit of fear but of power, love and of a sound mind." I repeated that scripture over and over and before I was aware, the radiation team was there to lower the table and undo the mask.

This went on for thirty five days. Chemotherapy went alongside the radiation. On the first day, I looked at the pack of chemo as it went through the tube into my veins and fell asleep for about five hours. I used to think I could control my strength, but chemo had me know that one's strength could be controlled unwillingly by substances. I had underestimated its effectiveness and considered it as ordinary drips of water. After each chemo, my hand could not even reach out for a glass of water close to my bed. I could not sit up on my own. I had to be supported by a nurse and taken out to the car on a wheelchair.

Once we arrived home I was taken straight to bed where I just slept. My mom would come around to see that I try to eat, but to no avail. I was throwing up everything I put in my mouth. Before starting my treatments, I thought I could only thank God for the food He provided, and it would be childish to say a prayer such as: "Dear Lord, thank you for strength to sit up, for the appetite to eat, for good taste and for the one who cooked the food."

When I started losing my taste and my throat became sore, I struggled to eat very little and could barely drink any liquid. One day I was really hungry and could not eat because I could no longer chew nor swallow anything. I could not imagine that I would crave food and smell its aroma and yet not be able to eat it.

This was too much. I had lost thirty five pounds out of a hundred and thirty five. I was all vegetables. Tears streamed down my face into my plate as I struggled to put scoops of food into my mouth. My parents reminded me of the fact that I had been strong; ever since I began taking the treatment I had been doing well. Besides that, I was almost done. They encouraged me to persevere until the end of everything.

Taste too is a luxury! Human beings are truly fearfully and wonderfully made. Everything about our bodies is so special. Life had become meaningless before starting the treatments and then I began to realize how special God had made every fiber of me. Sincere appreciation is profoundly made in the depreciation of one's condition.

It reached a point where I could no longer eat anything. That meant I could still thank God for the previous ability to chew, although painfully. "In everything give thanks for it is the will of God" (I Thessalonians 5:18). How was I going to thank God in such a tough situation? What had He done for me to thank Him? Well, sometimes it may seem useless in one's mind to thank Him but it would make sense to thank Him for yesterday when today is even worse. If your day is all bad, like people sometimes say it is, still thank God because He intended for it to be beautiful. Don't wait until it gets worse to thank Him for the "bad" times. In those times, remember that it could have been worse. Still, in the worst of times, He alone knows how to fix it.

Something needed to be done at this point lest I died! It was suggested that I have a peck tube inserted into my belly. That was the best option for me and so it was done. I could only be fed with water and Ensure milk through that tube for one hundred eighty days. Every time I felt hungry in the absence of the nurse, I called my mom to feed me through the tube. How did I look after six months without real food in my stomach? I looked pound-less. One windy day on our way somewhere, I was pushed by the wind and staggered greatly. I could have been knocked over by the breeze like a piece of paper if I had not held onto a metal object.

Who was going to do my laundry, feed me, etc. if my mom was not there? Every other person was at work. At the time my mom was the one who helped out in this area. I thank God for my caring mom. She is a very caring and loving person who deserves to be praised. I came to the realization that I had never appreciated my mother enough. It's not like I had never told her "thank you", but I realized that I needed to be more profound in my appreciation. It is one thing to thank someone because you know you ought to and it's another to thank them because you deeply know (feel the relief), recognize and appreciate that you have been helped when you needed it.

Every day should be "Mother's Day". Children sometimes miss the opportunity to thank their parents for the good work they have done in raising them. That concern spoke to my conscience as I watched my mother do everything for me tirelessly. She went as far as adjusting the pillows when I needed them moved. She stayed close by so she could hear my faint voice each time I called for help. With the tube, I could only sleep on a back-down position for six months. I had always slept on my stomach and it was hard for me to adapt, but I had no choice. It was such a great opportunity to be thankful to my mother. There I was, just lying on the bed. Wasn't I supposed to be helping my mom with the chores? Now it was the opposite and that was not a fair situation to see.

My sisters-in-law, Chrystelle and Nathalie, came to visit. Each time they cooked they tried to encourage me to eat, to no avail. A few days before their departure, Chrystelle cooked peanut nut stew and the aroma was flitting in the air. I told her, "That smells too good and I must eat. If it takes just putting it in my mouth and then going to throw it up each time it does not matter. I'll force myself to eat today". She was excited and as I struggled to eat, I realized that the stew got down my throat. She kept saying, "C'est ca Christine, il faut manger" meaning "There you go Christie, you have to eat." That was a good try. I had the sauce without the accompaniment, but that was a good step. Afterwards my feeding tube was cleaned and that day marked the beginning of a change as I started making an effort to eat other soft foods.

I could barely open my mouth and my wisdom teeth had to be taken out. I had to exercise my jaw bones with a therabite appliance continually until the opening of my mouth measured at least thirty millimeters. After mouth surgery, which was necessary to ease the opening of my mouth, I could open it comfortably at twenty-five millimeters. Extra work had to be done on my part under the monitoring of a mouth surgeon. I passed the test one day when it measured thirty millimeters exactly. The surgeon said I did not need a second surgery. Praise the Lord!

I began to feel a little more comfortable as I ate, so

99

it was time for the feeding tube to be removed. Patricia and I went to a different hospital this time. Shortly before I was called in, she stepped out to get something from the car. While inside, the doctor explained that he would remove the feeding tube by pulling it out. I thought he was going to anesthetize me just as they had done when it was inserted at the other hospital. He began to touch my stomach. I thought he was preparing for the procedure and before I looked at what he was doing, he pulled out the tube.

I wailed to the top of my voice. My wailing was unbelievable to him and he sunk down into his chair. I was wailing and saying, "This is wicked! This wicked! This is wicked! This hurts so badly, if only I knew what you were going to do, I would not have let you do this!" He sat there watching me until I calmed down. Afterwards, he gently took me down to the front entrance. As I stepped out, I met Patricia and in teary eyes I told her what happened. By the time she requested to see the practitioner in order to ask questions on how to deal with the pain, there was already someone else inside with him. We headed to the house and all I could do was lie on the bed and narrate the story to everyone. I could not move well and had to bend over in order to walk. The pain was excruciatingly high!

Chapter 10
Thank God, the Cancer is Gone!

After three rounds of chemotherapy, I had another scan to check if the cancer had shrunk. At my doctor's visit they analyzed the scan films and interpreted that the cancer was completely gone. They expected it to be reduced by 75%, but it was all gone.

I gave my testimony at church and the congregation was full of joy and amazement. I did not become blind. Instead, my eyesight was slowly restored. I had to move my entire head to look in any direction, because if I tilted only my eyes, my pupils stayed in one direction regardless of if I moved my body back to that position and it looked like my pupils were facing right while I was facing left.

Another time, I went to the doctor's office and a nurse was amazed at the look of my eyes and that I could hear more audibly. She started calling other nurses to come and see my eyes and a few doctors walked in to see how my pupils had readjusted. When Chrystelle took my braids out, she was so amazed at the length of my hair. It did not fall off and it was unusually longer than it had ever been.

God heard our agreement and had answered our prayer. His word shall not go out and return void, it will accomplish that which it was meant for. Patricia and I had agreed according to the word of God: "Again, I tell you that if two of you on earth agree about anything you ask for, it will be done for you by my Father in Heaven"

(Matthew 18:9). Like God promised, Patricia and I agreed that my hair was not going to fall off and it did not.

I made vows to God never to look at any obscene image with the eyes that He had given me. I began to thank God for my eyes that could see, ears that could hear, long hair, etc. It seemed to be a funny prayer to anyone who listened but I meant what I prayed about. I had taken those things for granted before but when I began to lose them, then I knew how desperately I needed them.

I thought I really had given up everything for Christ but what about my feet? Could I dance to any kind of song with them? I realized I was newly born again and had to start feeding my spirit more. It was a challenge through which I realized that one's best mentor as a new babe in Christ was the Holy Spirit and not people, no matter how long they have been in Christ and the titles they bore.

I had tried to model my spiritual walk with those who could quote Bible scriptures from cover to cover and failed to realize not everyone had been brought out of the pit that God had saved me from. My passion had to be different. After a few challenges and failures, I started allowing the Holy Ghost to be my mentor and began meditating on the word. After trying to spiritually walk with one born-again Christian I realized if human beings were solely in control of their walk in Christ, with no help from nor accountability to the Holy Ghost, they would fall.

The Christian walk is not about modeling your life after a certain preacher or someone who has a good mastery of Bible scriptures. It is sad to know that after some people truly surrender their lives to Christ, they depend on the mentorship of men who claim to be overly righteous or quote Bible scriptures. They tend to only believe what an imperfect human being under the cover of a title says. Just because a person carries a title or a so-called Evangelist tells them to lie at work so they can attend a Christian program, they would do it. They would do it with a sound conscience because they think the so-called Evangelist is their life conductor and everything he says is probably right to do; even if asked to steal, commit adultery or kill, they would do it. This is totally wrong!

If your Christian life is modeled according to another human being then you are bound to fall or find yourself worse than you were prior to becoming convicted of your sin. This is a true fact and I observed it myself while chatting with a few friends one day. One of my friends introduced me to another Christian brother. He was a good Bible scholar. However, I was a babe in Christ and my desire to learn about his passion for Christ grew, as I wanted to always hear him preach. Instead, he diverted the subject matter from God's love to a lustful desire. I found myself almost forgetting about what God had just done for me.

The Lord delivered me from this trap when a sister and brother in Christ reprimanded me for trying to compromise my faith. I quickly realized this was indeed a temptation from the enemy. I thank God for delivering me before the enemy's plans materialized. I learned the lesson that a Christian is blind without the spirit of discernment. Irrespective of age, mature Christians should keep an eye on whoever is teaching a newly saved Christian. As babes in Christ, they will eat whatever is served to them, whether good or poisoned. In fact, the character of God's messenger and the message they share should match.

Besides being part of the church, I began to read and study the word of God by myself. I asked the Holy Spirit to grant me understanding and revelation of the word and He did.

Some months later, I was privileged to meet Prophet Charles, who is a father in the Lord. He prophesied the word of God to me. In that prophesy the Lord told him to tell me not to believe every messenger just because they bore titles of Prophet, Apostle, Evangelist, etc. He told me to read the book of I John, which talks about testing spirits. I was so amazed that this word of prophecy addressed my previous ignorance. A few weeks later, I met a woman of God who prophesied the same word to me. She even went as far as telling my sister Patricia to keep an eye on those who came to minister to me. I believed the prophecy. Since then, I have been careful as to who is ministering to me. Also, the Lord has blessed me with great teachers of the word. Today, I also share the Gospel of Jesus Christ with anyone I feel led to, and souls are saved, people are healed and delivered.

Chapter 11
You Are Welcome to Confess to Jesus and Repent; Even You

If you are not conscious of the devil's temptations after you become saved and are not surrounded by spirit-filled Christians as a babe in Christ, the devil may embarrass you.

He may even come to you with the word of God like he came to Eve. In Genesis 3:1, "Now the serpent was more crafty than any of the wild animals the Lord God had made. He said to the woman, Did God really say you must not eat from any tree in the garden?" The devil paraphrased God's instruction. Eve may have been convinced by the serpent's words or she may have been swayed because he started off with the truth. If she had tested his spirit by the truth of God's word then she would have known his intentions.

It is in this same regard that some "titled" brethren search for terrains on which they can prove their ability in the word, then they vocalize their religious intentions to new babes in Christ, like I was. Don't be fooled. They can rightly quote all they want; saying how many times they have been on the pulpit, how long they can speak in tongues, how they can fast for many days, how they know the Greek version of the Bible, how many preachers they know, how many conferences they attend, how they approach certain situations, how their church settings are, how much they believe, etc. Don't be fooled. Religiosity sounds right but it is totally out of place. What about their self control, what about transparency and the fruits they bear?

Theory is easy even for the devil, but how real are we in our hearts? How many irrelevant theories have we preached and emphasized? One of mine used to be "it's not good to wear jeans on Sunday". Let's check ourselves and name a few:

1. _____

2. _____

3. _____

4. _____

5. _____

I asked God to forgive me and to touch the hearts of those I had hurt. He then touched the hearts of some people I had terribly hurt and they forgave me. From them, I then learned to forgive those who had hurt me. Nevertheless, I was not forgiven to stay in silence. I was forgiven so I could encourage others to choose forgiveness. If we confess our sins, He is faithful and just to forgive us. It is not enough to only confess; we must also repent and seek the wisdom and guidance of the Holy Spirit.

What evil thing are we asking Jesus to help us stop? What are we doing that is hidden in the eyes of the church?

If we say we have not sinned, the Bible calls us liars. Let us ask God to give us new hearts:

Father, _____

_____

_____

_____

_____

_____

The Holy Spirit will convict us of our actions and by the grace of God, we will do the right thing. Maybe we want to stop being envious of someone we claim to know and love yet refuse to share even our testimonies with them. In our minds we know they are a good person and spirit-filled, but envy, pride, etc. have found a seat in our hearts. All we do is wait for someone to speak a little evil of them and we spew out hateful thoughts, forgetting how they had been there for us. Indeed, it is only the grace of God that helps us to love others.

The Bible says the human heart is desperately wicked, but it did not say it should remain that way. It is written, "Let this mind be in you which was also in Christ Jesus" (Philippians 2:5).

I used to be the quiet person who swallowed every angry thought when people did not speak nicely to me. It was such an issue in the pit my belly that eventually resulted in resentment and hatred towards some people. My quietness covered everything up. Some said I was truly humble, not knowing there was a bitter Christie inside. Quietness meant obedience and humility to me at one time. No one knew how far I wanted to fly, how much I wanted to spank and just blow up at someone.

A lot of bitterness was growing inside of me. I thought I could rid myself of it when I did what I wanted and had my opinion aired a few times, but truly we have to call a spade by its name and ask God for His grace to help us forgive. Some of cancer's nourishment is in the dirtiness of one's heart. Sometimes I was stressed but never knew how to deal with it. Now that the air I breathe has become precious to me, by God's grace, I have made the choice to be free through Jesus.

Were you ever told you could never handle anything right? Did you believe that lie? What about you? Do you still bear the stigma of what you did years ago even after you repented? Are you waiting for someone to apologize? Do not wait for them, move forward and ask Jesus to heal your heart. Don't wait for apologies that delay and don't expect applause after you choose to forgive. Make the choice for the sake of your own health and peace. Allow the Holy Ghost to lead you and take you to your destined place in Christ Jesus. It feels good to be set free from Satan's bondage. Jesus Christ is the choice to make.

Chapter 12
It's Cancer Again; Oh Lord, Help

I went to a few gatherings where I danced to secular songs, to the selfish satisfaction of my flesh. I must confess that was not healthy for my spirit. That was me and I don't know about you.

Later, my right leg started hurting badly and I began to limp. I assumed I had merely hurt my leg but when I tried to turn on the bed one night, it felt like my joint had been dislocated. It hurt so badly that I started weeping "oh, oh, oh, oh" it was such a sharp pain.

I thought I was sobbing silently so I wouldn't disturb anyone's sleep, but shortly after, Patricia and Raymond were in my room to find out what was happening. "It's my leg", I cried. I did not want anyone to touch it. It felt as if I was on pins and needles. They asked if I needed some ice on it. In teary eyes, I told them not to worry about it. I wanted them to go back to their room and let me cry alone but they did not go until they prayed and saw that I stopped crying. Just because I stopped crying did not mean the pain went away. I kept whispering to myself, "Oh God, what is this again?"

It was morning when I had to deal with it again and I called to make an appointment with my doctor who told me to come in immediately. Another scan was requested and cancer of the hip bone was evident. It was agreed that I would have 22 radiation therapy treatments. I told myself if God dealt with the first cancer then I evidently knew the outcome of this one too.

I made a vow to God again that I would never use my legs to dance to musical lyrics that didn't please Him. The Holy Spirit started making me sensitive to the kinds of songs that caused me to ignore Him and pay attention to my flesh. Though they popped up in my mind sometimes, I confessed for even thinking about them or trying to whistle their notes; because as soon as I started, it ushered my mind elsewhere. In 22 days, I was finished with the treatment.

One morning, I got a phone call from one of my uncles who started the conversation by asking me why I was sick. His next question was, "Christie, what did you do?" Well, if I did anything so bad that no other person had ever done then I deserved to be sick. That's exactly how I interpreted his question. In his prayer for me he said, "Lord, there are older people in the family that could understandably be sick, not this child." When he said "Amen" I regretted that I had agreed in prayer with him.

Sometimes people have to be careful about what they say in their prayers and how and with whom they make agreements. My uncle forgot that he was very much older than I and that the older person he suggested could be sick in my place, according to his prayer, could be him. Not too long after our conversation, I was told he was in the hospital. Hey, I echoed to myself, "What had he done to be there?" I was not supposed to ask this but imaginarily, I was reiterating his question back to him. He had mentioned in his prayer that my situation would have been justified if it had involved an older person. He was saying that out of compassion, but sincere compassion always wants the situation to go away, not for someone else to suffer pain in another person's place.

Pain is pain, whether one is young or old. I was told of a fifteen year old relative whose left leg had been amputated because cancer had spread to it. I felt so sorry for the young boy and prayed that God would take him through the tough times, but I never wished for some other person to go through that pain instead of him.

My uncle asked what I did wrong to deserve cancer. Job's situation made his friends think he had offended God. Job himself thought God was punishing him. Job 19:21 says, "Have pity on me, my friends, have pity, for the hand of God has struck me." Unknowingly, Job had falsely accused God of striking him. The devil was the one behind all of Job's troubles. God was not punishing him, it was Satan's intention to have him suffer.

Look at Job 2:3-10: "Then the Lord said to Satan, Have you considered my servant Job? There is no one on earth like him; he is blameless and upright, a man who fears God and shuns evil. And he still maintains his integrity, though you incited me against him to ruin him without any reason. Skin for skin! Satan replied. A man will give all he has for his own life. But stretch out your hand and strike his flesh and bones, and surely he will curse you to your face. The Lord said to Satan, Very well, then he is in your hands; but you must spare his life. So Satan went out from the presence of the Lord and afflicted Job with painful sores from the soles of his feet to the top of his head. Then Job took a piece of broken pottery and scraped himself with it as he sat among the ashes. His wife said to him, Are you still holding on to your integrity? Curse God

111

and die! He replied, You are talking like a foolish woman. Shall we accept good from God, and not trouble? In all this, Job did not sin in what he said."

People are not always sick because they sinned. If that were the case everyone would be sick. God does not punish us in proportion to our sins. If He were to do so, not one soul would be living on planet earth. The Lord shows mercy to whosoever He pleases. Sometimes we think we can quantify His mercy, but it is written in Isaiah 55:8-9, "For my thoughts are not your thoughts, neither are your ways my ways, declares the Lord. As the heavens are higher than the earth, so are my ways higher than your ways and my thoughts than your thoughts." No matter what the magnitude of our situation is, it is our place to seek God's mercy because it is always available.

God's mercy does not give us the freedom to sin. Just as someone's love, gentleness, kindness, patience or virtue of any kind should not be taken for a weakness; neither should we keep sinning intentionally just because His grace and mercy are available.

Repentance is an important part of our Christian walk. God grants us the grace to stop doing those things for which He has forgiven us. He wants us to realize how slow He is in anger and how abundant He is in love. We are warned in the scriptures about the dangers of continual sin. Jesus even told the woman caught in adultery to go and sin no more.

The mercy of God may also come with chastisement. You might get away with crossing through the red traffic light and the mercy of God may have been upon you. If you cultivate the practice of always crossing the red traffic light, God may allow you to be caught by a law enforcement officer. Not only does the Lord want you to suffer the consequences of getting a ticket, but most of all He is protecting you from an accident that might have caused you to be lame for the rest of your life. Refusing to repent can invite calamity to come your way.

Chapter 13
Take the Time to Say "Thank You Lord"

The LORD has been so merciful and kind that He deserves all our praises. That is why as believers we should give thanks in everything we do. Jesus healed ten lepers yet only one came back to thank him. What about us? Did we also just walk away after getting what we wanted? Could I have walked away after God healed me?

Confession of sin became a daily routine and I felt relieved each time I let go of hatred towards people. Bitterness and joy do not mesh. One cannot harbor bitterness, unforgiveness and peace at the same time. It's impossible and so one will dominate the other.

Were there times when I felt I was alone? Yes I did! I always used to call my mother to come so we could converse while I was on my sick bed. Sometimes she had nothing to say but she would sing praises to God which lulled me to sleep. I realized life was about spending time with people and loving them. I could not do much on that sick bed but become conscious of the fact that God had been my strength throughout my life and He needed my attention more than ever before.

I got a phone call from my brother Sampson and we prayed. After our conversation ended I was so amazed about how he expressed his love for Christ in such a holy exuberance. It never dawned on me to ask him when he became born again.

In another conversation, he recounted that when he was unable to see me at the airport during my stop in Paris, he went home and turned on the television. A Christian program was on the air. He watched a man who had cancer and the way that man looked made him feel so bad and he thought I was soon going to have the same experience after my treatment.

Later, he made the choice of surrendering his life to Christ. He felt convicted that if he did not accept Christ and start living the way God wanted him to live, I might die. Thereafter, he went right ahead and bought a Bible. He did not understand what he was reading so the next thing he did was look for a Bible-based church where he fellowshipped. Though he surrendered his life for fear that I could die, he later understood that God loves us and wants us saved.

I was so touched by his story and began to understand one of the many reasons why God had allowed me to endure my hardship. It could not be understood while I was sick but God shapes destiny through some hard situations. The goodness which came out of my situation was not only for my benefit but for my family and friends as well; most of them reconsidered appreciating God for life.

Chapter 14
Jesus is the Only Star

I had been indoors for a long time and wanted to get out of the house, so Patricia registered me in an editing class led by one of the women in the church. As I walked around the media center where we worked, I saw a calendar that caught my attention. On it were the months of the year that accompanied the horoscope signs. Right away the Holy Ghost reminded me of my childhood days when I confessed that I was "Cancer" because I was born in June. It may not sound reasonable but cancer is the word and its many meanings can be manifested through anyone who called it upon themselves. The Bible says life and death lies in the power of the tongue and those who love it will eat its fruit.

In the book of Matthew, the journey to the birth place of Jesus is said to be the only time whereby the magi followed the star that led them to Jesus. Horoscopes are termed to be stars but Jesus is the only true star and there is no other star (savior) under which we live and move and have our being. More so, God has given human beings dominion over the fowls of the air, the animals and over every other living creature.

In disagreement with the horoscopes, why would we condescend to being classified under titles named after animals (Capricorn, Sagittarius, Aquarius, Gemini, Leo) etc? Why would we accept false prophesies designated by people we do not know, who predict we will have a bad day according to their capacity to read the stars? The Bible says, "For we know in part and we prophesy in part", which is the truth, so how can these horoscopes tell people about themselves and their lives every week? We don't live under the dispensation of luck. Nothing happens by chance. Even when a coin is flipped, the side on which it falls was already known by God. He is the Alpha and the Omega and He knows the end from the beginning.

Jesus does not hide himself. He tells us that He is the way, the truth and the life and no one can go to the Father except through Him. Most, if not all, of the time people do not even know who wrote the horoscopes they believe in. How can you believe a prophet you do not know? Who revealed those messages to them about you? If the plan is not from God then it is a lie. Amos 3:7 says, "Surely the sovereign Lord does nothing without revealing his plan to his servants the prophets."

Oftentimes the horoscopes describe what happened in the lives of celebrities or high standing people in society, after which those occurrences are matched to what they think will also happen to someone born in the same month. It's ludicrous that people believe they will have the same experience or personality type as someone else simply because they share the same birth month. After having these convictions, I thought how ignorant I had been to have accepted such things. The Bible says, "My people are destroyed for lack of knowledge" (Hosea 4:6).

Suspicion will set in if you give room to it. A woman once told Patricia that I had been sick because a friend had consulted a witch doctor on my behalf. My sister told her, "That is not one bit true", which ended that conversation. Sometimes, people do not come to your aid when you are sick and in need of help. All they are interested in is telling you about the evil that runs through their minds.

Another time Patricia was told by a different woman that she should find out why I'm sick from fortunetellers. This woman suggested I had been sick because I lived in places I should not have. She opted to take my sister to one of her fortunetellers. Before she could finish what she had to say, my sister told her that we had never believed and would never believe in such things.

My cousin, some friends and I attended a wedding in Texas. I was not interested in the music so my friends kept asking if I was okay sitting down and I told them "yes". They could not believe I would sit down while the latest hot sounds played. Well, it was not by my power, nor might, but it was by the Holy Spirit that I sat down. I did not dance in my spirit either. They failed to understand that they would not have had the opportunity to ask me why I was not dancing if I did not have legs. Does that mean we should not dance? No! I was just not interested in that genre of music.

I was told that one of my other cousins was looking for me in the crowd so I started looking for her too. We had not seen each other in about twenty years. Finally when I saw her, she was so amazed and told me that she had been in search of a lame girl. She thought I would at least be limping or something. I laughed as she expressed her surprise at how good I looked. It was indeed a miracle to her. She took me around as she told her friends, "This girl is a walking miracle".

The next day, we went to my cousin Sheila's church, Omega Gospel Ministries, Texas. The pastor asked that newcomers introduce themselves. I was the only visitor that Sunday and I found myself giving my testimony. I noticed people were so captivated and the pastor asked me to come out and gave me five extra minutes to share my testimony. When I finished, the congregation gave God a standing ovation with such awesome enthusiasm.

When I returned to my seat someone asked if I had been on any of the Christian television networks to give my testimony. "No", I replied, "I share my story with whoever the Holy Ghost leads me to; anytime, anywhere". After service, the pastor asked if it was okay for me to give my testimony on DAYSTAR Television. Together with another pastor, we went to the studio and I had the opportunity to share my testimony briefly.

On my way back to Nevada, I sat beside a lady to whom I testified. I told her about the healing power of Jesus and she said she was convicted to throw her cigarettes away. I told her if she was convicted by the fact that cigarettes were not good for her then she should follow what she had in mind. She kept insisting that as soon as we got off the plane, she would throw them away. Well, I had not suggested she throw out her cigarettes. All I did was tell her about the healing power of God. Her urge to throw them away could only come from the Holy Ghost. Only the Holy Ghost has the power to convict anyone about anything.

Chapter 15

Leave Your Belongings in Egypt; There are Better Things in the "Promised Land"

Have you ever grumbled about the things you missed doing and what you thought you had lost? Occasionally, part of us thinks back to where we would have been if life's trials hadn't come and changed the course of our well-laid plans. I was in the Advanced School of Mass Communication when cancer struck and everything came to a standstill. Honestly, I cried sometimes when looking back at what I missed, but the Holy Ghost convicted me during those sentimental moments; after which, I confessed and asked for forgiveness.

Sometimes God allows time and space for you to have those thoughts to see if you really are grateful for what He has done in you. It also gives you the opportunity to see how much trust you have in Him. If He just saved your soul from going to hell or your mortal body from going to the grave, isn't that enough to be thankful for?

What about my dreams? Yes, I probably would have finished school by now but if He who has the power to promote allows me to be delayed, as described in the view of men, wouldn't He also promote me again? God is able to do exceeding abundantly above what we think or even ask (Ephesians 3:20) and His plans for us are good and not evil, to give us an expected end (Jeremiah 29:11). We make plans on our own but the reply comes from the

Lord. No one ever takes a step forward without God knowing about it first.

Sometimes we credit ourselves for the beautiful outcome of things in our lives and think we have them because of our hard work. It's so easy to forget that God is watching us like someone who is watching a tape. He has the remote control in hand to forward, rewind or pause a scenario. If the person who has the remote control decides to rewind or forward the tape and it does not work, the indication may be that the tape is out of order. It's in the same manner that God has the ability to decide to bring us back, promote us or allow us to die.

We may rebelliously try to fight the plan of God in our lives but He will always prevail. Whether we want it or not and whether we like it or not, God will do what He said He will do. So it is not time to worry or grumble because His word asks, "Which of us by worrying can add a single hour to his life?" (Matthew 6:25-27)

It would not matter if you were stopped close to the end of medical school. It would not matter if you were the one the nation was counting on to win the golf or tennis tournament. It would not matter if the massive audience was waiting for you to shoot your telecast. It would not matter if you were on the verge of following up to get that million dollar house. It would not matter if you were preparing for your wedding. It just would not matter if God had to bring any agenda of ours to a standstill just to get us to listen to His voice.

When Sodom and Gomorrah were in ashes, Lot, his wife and two daughters were blessed to be the only ones whom God spared. They were all commanded not to look back as they moved forward. They probably heard the crumbling sounds of the buildings as they burned down and thought to look back. If some of us were placed in the same situation, we would have perhaps thought of the beautiful houses, our bank account information, the acres of land, etc. Lot's wife did not realize it was better for her to escape death empty handed as she thought of looking behind. Instead of thanking God for saving her, she preoccupied her mind with thoughts of what was left behind. When those thoughts caused her to look back, she turned into a pillar of salt.

After the tragic attacks on the United States on September 11 the Twin Towers collapsed to Ground Zero, yet the loss of buildings didn't draw our tears. We cried for the victims. Ask a survivor what they cared about most when everything was falling apart. Surely, they would say they cried out for their life. Life itself is more valuable than possessions and cannot be reduced to merely attaining our desired accomplishments.

When Hurricane Katrina threatened the state of Texas, most people were doing everything they could to evacuate because of what they had seen of Katrina's effects in Louisiana. In the time of a storm, what matters most is your life. If you are still living after it's over you should be thanking God. When the storm was raging, you did not want anything but for God to save your life and that of your family, so don't worry about what was lost while in the midst of it.

In my convalescent phase, I remember not going to church on some Sundays because I was frustrated and angry after trying on several outfits and none of them seemed to fit. I had lost 35 pounds and weighed only 100 pounds. I said, "Now nothing fits me; everything, skirts, shirts, dresses do not fit anymore." I had quickly forgotten about the day I was so weak that I went to the hospital wearing my pajamas. It did not matter to me at the time. What mattered was getting there to receive the treatment.

I wrote this poem in my solitude, titled *I Don't Mind!*

I LOVE MYSELF
I WOULD NEVER WISH TO BE SOMEONE ELSE
CONTENT WITH LIFE'S SITUATIONS
BEATEN BY CANCER SEVERAL TIMES
I AM A CONQUEROR IN JESUS!

I LOOK AROUND
AND NO RAY OF HOPE SHINES AT TWENTY-FIVE,
IN MY HURTFUL BLISS
I FEEL MY PAIN ALONE
LIKE AN IMPRISONED CHILD
IN THIS WORLD OF TRAGEDIES
I DON'T MIND
I AM A CONQUEROR IN JESUS!

FEARLESS OF EVERY HAPPENING
ONE DAY I'LL OVERCOME
CHRISTIE IS MY NAME
AND A CHRISTIAN WILL I REMAIN
TILL ETERNITY CALLS ME CLOSE
I DON'T MIND
I AM A CONQUEROR THROUGH JESUS!

I DON'T FEAR ANYMORE
I DON'T FEAR DEATH, CANCER, NOR STORMS
THEY ALL COME AND PASS
THE REASON THEY DON'T LAST IS BECAUSE,
I DON'T MIND!
I AM A CONQUEROR THROUGH JESUS!!!

I was asked to present one of my poems in church one night and I chose "I DON'T MIND". I was amazed that I went back to my seat with tears in my eyes. Sometimes conquerors cry not because they feel defeated but because the situation is painful, yet still they know that they are more than conquerors.

Chapter 16
Beautiful?

After my treatment, I looked in the mirror and noticed my face was so black it could only be compared to charcoal as it was flaking. As long as I could see, nothing else mattered. The possibility of becoming blind after the treatment had traumatized me so much that after God healed my sight, I had another definition of beauty. Unlike before when facial appearance concluded my judgment, this time beauty meant appreciating God for good health. Nothing is as bad as having eyes that cannot see or ears that cannot hear. I still was fearfully and wonderfully made. Ugly was not in my mind. I knew that I had experienced an awesome miracle and that was more than beautiful.

Some have cultivated the habit of criticizing other people's physical appearance as well as their own. Some have thought: if only my eyes were a little smaller, if only my nose was not so long, if only I had a round face, if only I did not have these rabbit-sized ears, etc. Some people have become familiar with their critical attitude so much so that it has veiled their sense of right and wrong. The truth is when one does that, they criticize the wonderful artwork of the Lord and insult God's image because we all were created in His image. Genesis 1:27 says, "So God created man in His own image, in the image of God He created him; male and female He created them."

Sometimes we may not look as good as we'd like, but the truth of the matter is no human being should be termed "ugly" and no one should think they are "ugly".

Jehovah Elohim, the God of creation, tells us that we are fearfully and wonderfully made (Psalm 139:14). That is the way we are supposed to see ourselves. God created us in His image and that is what is most beautiful.

God wants us to recognize that He knows each one of us completely. No child lives with his parents and does not recognize their voice, and vice versa. No good parent tolerates a child who hears and never listens to instruction. God's word says that to spare the rod is to spoil the child. I said I was God's child and claimed to obey Him, but God requires more than just professing to be born-again. He wants us to obey His word in our everyday lives.

I heard and obeyed God more when I was sick. We can hear God speak more through His word when we are feeble, when we are sleeping, unable to talk and when we are helpless. God acts in uncertain situations and His mystery and beauty are manifested in ways we do not expect. Hannah prayed and cried until she could talk no more and when the priest saw her, he thought she was drunk. Later on she was blessed to give birth to the prophet Samuel.

Let's not take the gentle voice of the Holy Spirit for granted. Though the Lord chastises those whom He loves, it does not feel good. The voice of the Holy Spirit seems louder after we have fallen short but it is the same gentle voice that warns before any dreadful situation comes our way. The only reason why the same gentle voice which comforts, counsels and teaches seems louder is because most often we tend to give more attention to the one who can solve our problems when faced with a serious challenge. A child who was told by the mom not to touch the icing on the cake heard the warning better after he tried to touch it and was reprimanded.

As human beings, we all have searched for beauty in places where it does not reside. We have looked at just the superficial part, but what about the integral part where our spirit comes into play? Our true beauty is revealed through our obedience to God's word and our patience for the manifestation of His promises.

Chapter 17
Are You Sick Today?

You may be on your sickbed today, but sometimes all you need to hear is someone else's testimony. My friend's mother, Aunty Magdalene heard about my testimony and her hope was strengthened by it. With an amazing assurance, she confessed that she was going to make it through her cancer treatment by the same power of Jesus. Several times, I have been blessed to share my testimony with cancer patients who always draw courage from what Jesus did for me.

Testimonies give birth to new testimonies. They were not meant to be shelved. After Jesus Christ performed miracles, many unbelievers believed in Him. Spreading the good news of the gospel is all about testifying about the goodness of Jesus, which will ultimately create new testimonies as souls are saved and lives are changed by the power of the Lord.

It is not the doctor's fault that he gives an upsetting report. If he can rightly diagnose what the problem is and call out the name of the sickness, then praise the Lord for that.

Jesus himself asked the oppressed man what his name was and he answered, "My name is legion, for we are many." The disciples were unable to cast some demons out and they called for Jesus to help. Jesus told them the demons would not come out except through prayer and fasting. Sometimes our situations look impossible no matter how much we pray. We need other Christians to fast and pray on our behalf when we are weak and unable.

Chapter 18
Don't Worry, It Is Finished

It is always good to have a self check when going through tough situations. It helps me and I suggest these for everyone.

1. Are you thinking more about the bad report?

2. Are you surrounded by grief-stricken people?

3. Do you think you are more afflicted than others?

4. Are you crying more than praying and listening to music full of God's hope?

5. Are you blaming others and your past or are you forgiving yourself, other people and surrendering all to God?

6. Are you surrounded by people who are saying you deserve what you are going through? Do you agree with them?

For every sick person, Jesus is asking: "Would you be made whole?" Believing you can be made whole is trusting that Jesus loves you so much that He died, was buried and rose again to save you. He is now seated at the right hand of God the Father Almighty.

This summarized message of the cross at Calvary portrays Jesus as the overcomer of all sickness, stress, sin, etc. By a Christian's heavenly right, nothing—absolutely nothing—no sickness or peril can separate you from the love of God (Romans 8:35-39). He loved us even before we loved Him. If our earthly fathers can give us nice things then how much more can we expect from our heavenly Father?

Think it through. I wish we could be brave and not cry. It is okay to cry, but after drying your tears, just remember: *Jehovah* is our Creator, *Jehovah-Rapha* is our Healer, *Jehovah-Shalom* is our Peace, *Jehovah-Tsidkenu* is our Righteousness, *Jehovah-Maccaddeshem* is our Sanctification, *Jehovah-Nissi* is our Banner, *Jehovah-Shammah* is the One who is ever present, *Adonai* is our Master, *El-Shaddai* is God Almighty, our sufficiency. God is the great I AM.

He loves us and has promised never to leave nor forsake us: the One who calms the waves and the seas, the One whom death obeys, the One who holds the keys of death and life and no one goes into or out of any of these transitions without His permission. He is the One to whom every knee will bow and every tongue confess that Jesus Christ is Lord. He is the One who will come to judge the quick (living) and the dead. He is in control of every situation and can do what human beings, modern science, insights, plans, intelligence and earthly wisdom cannot accomplish.

Do you believe that Jesus died and rose again for you and that He is sitting at the right hand of God the Father Almighty? Everyone has the choice.

Do you believe in the healing power of the blood of Jesus?

Do you believe that He who raised Lazarus from the dead is still the same and He can bring your hopeless situation to life?

No matter how bad the situation may seem; have you tried Jesus? If you called on Him, let Him have His way because He is THE WAY, THE TRUTH and THE LIFE and no one goes to the Father except by Him. Remember, it is a personal choice to have faith in either death or life and the word of God advices us to choose life. I encourage you to choose life as well.

My prayer of agreement for you:

Dear Father,

I humbly come before your throne of grace in total surrender. I believe that you are the King of Kings and Lord of Lords over my life. You are the one and only true living God.

Forgive all of my iniquities and wash me white as snow with the precious blood of Jesus. By your word which does not go out and come back void, you were wounded for our transgressions, bruised for our infirmities, and the chastisement of our peace was upon you. By your stripes we are healed.

In Jesus' name I believe that you died, were buried and rose again and now sit at the right hand of God the Father Almighty. I believe that you are coming back to judge the world.

You who healed Christiana, please heal me today. Not because of my prayer but because of your mercy, grace and power you are able to do exceeding and abundantly above what I think or even ask. What is impossible with man is possible with you. As I claim my healing, I thank you Lord for what you have done. I can never repay you for all that you have done for me. Teach me your ways and empower me to follow you until this world passes away.

Until then,

Amen

My Favorite Healing Scriptures

Isaiah 53:5 (NIV)

"But He was pierced for our transgressions, he was crushed for our iniquities; the punishment that brought us peace was upon Him, and by his wounds we are healed."

3 John 1:2 (NIV)

"Dear friend, I pray that you may enjoy good health and that all may go well with you, even as your soul is getting along well."

James 5:13-15 (NIV)

"Is any among you in trouble? He should pray. Is anyone happy? Let him sing songs of praise. Is any one of you sick? He should call the elders of the church to pray over him and anoint him with oil in the name of the Lord. And the prayer offered in faith will make the sick person well; the Lord will raise him up. If he has sinned, he will be forgiven. Therefore confess your sins to each other and pray for each other so that you may be healed. The prayer of a righteous man is powerful and effectual."

Jeremiah 17:14 (NIV)

"Heal me, O Lord, and I will be healed; save me and I will be saved, for you are the one I praise."

Proverbs 15:30 (NIV)

"A cheerful look brings joy to the heart, and good news gives health to the bones."

2 Chronicles 7:14 (NIV)

"If my people which are called by my name shall humble themselves and pray and seek my face and turn from their wicked ways, then will I hear from heaven, and forgive their sin, and will heal their land."

Deuteronomy 32:39 (ESV)

"See now that I, even I, am he, and there is no god beside me; I kill and I make alive; I wound and I heal; and there is none that can deliver out of my hand."

SPREAD THE GOOD NEWS THAT JESUS HEALS.

Notes about your Journey:

_____

_____

_____

_____

_____

_____

_____

_____

_____

_____

_____

_____

_____

_____

_____

_____

_____

_____

_____

_____

_____

_____

_____

_____
_____
_____
_____
_____
_____
_____
_____
_____
_____
_____
_____
_____
_____
_____
_____
_____
_____
_____
_____
_____
_____
_____
_____

Thank You Father

www.ingramcontent.com/pod-product-compliance
Lightning Source LLC
LaVergne TN
LVHW021345080426
835508LV00020B/2125